"*Unwanted Advances* is necessary. Argue with the author, by all means. But few people have taken on the excesses of university culture with the brio that Kipnis has."

—Jennifer Senior, *New York Times*

"...s searching account by a feminist scholar explores the ex-...nces of professors caught up in Kafkaesque inquisitions, ...ated in Laura Kipnis's case simply by her objecting to the ...ding of others. She laments an age when risky ideas, rather ...eing embraced in the university, are being chased out."

— *...ll Street Journal* Top 10 Non-Fiction Books of the Year 2017

"...ry, pragmatic analysis . . . The greatest pleasure *Unwanted ...ces* affords comes from Kipnis's keen sense of human ...ology."

—*Bookforum*

"...nis has written a brave, disturbing, yet scrupulously fair ...: a brilliant and pragmatic manifesto for a kind of 'adult' ...nism that rejects the campus cult of female victimhood."

—Terry Castle, author of *The Professor*

"...nis is everything the academic bureaucrats she writes ...out are not: brave, honest, judicious, mature, and self- ...with a seasoned understanding of both sexual politics ...mpus politics. She has struck a mighty blow for sanity, ..., and academic freedom."

—William Deresiewicz, author of *Excellent Sheep*

"na...ling, shocking, meticulously reported, eminently readable, ...n places perversely hilarious . . . most of all it is a crucial ...f a burgeoning conversation about threats to free speech ...ellectual freedom on coll... ...rion as her insights are a..."

—Meghan I...

"Laura Kipnis's new book is a revelation: a great work of investigative journalism and a thorough examination of a case that feels like it couldn't happen in America . . . Kipnis makes you fear for a whole new set of reasons."

—Hanna Rosin, author of *The End of Men*

"This book is harrowing; this book is hilarious (like Dorothy Parker channelling Franz Kafka); but the main thing it is is BRAVE. On top of which, it is urgently necessary."

—Lawrence Weschler, author of *Waves Passing in the Night*

"Force[s] readers to really consider their position and to see if they can fully defend it, or at least to think beyond feminist platitudes ... a persuasive and valuable contribution to the continuing debate over how to deal with sexual assault on college campuses."

—Jill Filipovic, *New York Times Book Review*

"Riveting read . . . a bracing book, its message delivered with fierce intelligence and mordant humor."

—*Bookshelf*

"Clarity of expression and the uncompromising vehemence of her thoughts make Kipnis the best polemical investigator writing today, which both sells her short and raises an unexpected question: how come reading her, however uncomfortable or complex the subject, is always such a tremendous pleasure?"

—Geoff Dyer, author of *White Sands*

"Rather brilliant."

—Andy Martin, *Independent*

"Laura Kipnis is a hero. She has written a book that will benefit many while bringing all kinds of grief upon her."

—Bob Ostertag, *Huffington Post*

"The author's trenchant yet witty analysis reveals how the entrance of university administrators, each with his or her own agendas and vendettas, rendered a complex situation even murkier and more byzantine . . . As in all her books, Kipnis is consistently provocative and intelligent."

—*Kirkus*

"Courageous, thought-provoking ... Without diminishing the gravity of sexual assault, Kipnis's readable and judiciously reported work illustrates how the 'sex-as-danger preoccupation on campuses now' is infantilizing women rather than empowering them."

—*Publishers Weekly*

"A bracing book, its message delivered with fierce intelligence and mordant humor."

—Cathy Young, *Wall Street Journal*

"Teaches us another important lesson about how to confront pressing issues without foreclosing engaging argumentation, constraining critical distance or letting the discourse devolve into moralizing."

—James Anderson, *Heterodox Academy*

"It's hard to imagine an objective reader finishing *Unwanted Advances* and not having her mind changed, if she has up to now accepted the mainstream version we've been reading in the news: that Title IX is a necessary tool to safeguard women who have been sexually assaulted . . . A clarion call for both men and women to recognize the reality of female autonomy that feminism has always argued for, and that today's campus culture threatens to eclipse."

—David Mikics, *Tablet*

Unwanted Advances

SEXUAL PARANOIA COMES TO CAMPUS

Laura Kipnis

VERSO

First published in the UK by Verso 2018

1 3 5 7 9 10 8 6 4 2

Verso
UK: 6 Meard Street, London W1F 0EG
US: 20 Jay Street, Suite 1010, Brooklyn, NY 11201
versobooks.com

Verso is the imprint of New Left Books

ISBN-13: 978-1-78873-257-4
ISBN-13: 978-1-78873-258-1 (UK EBK)

British Library Cataloguing in Publication Data
A catalogue record for this book is available from the British Library

Printed and bound by CPI Group (UK) Ltd, Croydon, CR0 4YY

For Myra, Nancypants, and little Lans

Contents

Author's note

The people I've named in the book are those who've given me permission to use their names. I've also named public figures and those involved in these events in an official capacity (some of whose names have already been made public in lawsuits anyway). I've changed the names of students, and others who prefer not to be named. I've also changed the names of a few people I'd otherwise fear running into on my campus.

Preface to the UK Edition: #MeToo and Campus Sexual Paranoia

At first, it was a lot of enormous media potentates crashing to earth, followed by a bunch of lesser despots and lords (many also employed in the media industries), which soon expanded to include half the men in Hollywood and ancillary trades like politics. The accompanying din was the clamor of pundits (those who hadn't yet been felled themselves) attempting to explain what had happened—then reexplain, then explain some more—because the picture kept changing: soon the not-so-powerful were under fire, too (freelance writers and experimental novelists were among those anonymously charged in an online list of "shitty men"), and it was becoming unclear whether it was "toxic masculinity" or masculine panic we were talking about.

But at the beginning, the story seemed plain enough. It turns out that in the tallest skyscrapers and plushest hotels of the most advanced economies, many high-profile men have been acting the part of feudal lords, demanding droit de seigneur from their vassals, the vassals in this case being their female employees and others wishing entry into the lordly fiefdoms. Evidently there's been a covert system of taxation on female advancement in the work world, with the unluckier among us obligated to render not just the usual fealty demanded by overweening bosses but varying degrees of sexual homage too, from ego-stroking and fluffing (which is gross enough), to being grabbed and groped, to the expectation of silence about full-on rape.

From a political standpoint the exposés about the current extent of sexual harassment look like a significant cultural up-heaval: a major victory in the centuries-long fight for women's equality. This time the battleground was the workplace, and the opponents being slain the career gatekeepers. A struggle over careers is, to be sure, a bourgeois revolution—I mean this in the historical rather than the disparaging sense. If women's bodies are still being treated as property, then another Reign of Terror was long overdue. If women are stuck with the task of overthrow-ing aristocratic privilege a few hundred years late, it's because this social stratum needs to be liquidated before all genders can achieve civic and economic equality.

That the agents of destruction have been women simply tell-ing their stories in public is nothing less than delicious. Women were gossiping, complaining, name-calling, and suddenly the world was listening. (In fact, historians have written extensively on the importance of gossip and its venues, such as coffeehouses and taverns, in fomenting previous revolutions.) Each tale that came tumbling out was more sordid than the last: infinite varia-tions on the theme of sexual scumminess. The revelations weren't exactly new, but the frame had shifted: the handsy boss, the lewd entreaties, the casting couch were no longer going to be busi-ness as usual. Every revolution has its weapons of choice—once it was muskets and guillotines, this time around it's "sharing" and media exposure. It wasn't heads that were rolling, it was liveli-hoods: contracts yanked, deals canceled, agents quitting, e-mail accounts shuttered. But career death is hardly nothing—it's the modern equivalent of losing everything.

When the *New York Times* compiled a photo gallery of prominent men accused of sexual harassment (currently over seventy
names), it did rather bring to mind the spectacle of heads on
a pike in a public square. The name conspicuously absent, unfortunately, was our current groper-in-chief Donald Trump,
who's thus far managed to slither away from the variety of sexual
charges lodged against him. (Though perhaps by the time you
read this ...)

About those chopped-down potentates and lords. Many, one
couldn't help but notice (especially at the beginning), were not
the most attractive specimens on the block: bulbous, jowly men;
fat men who told women they needed to lose weight; ugly men
drawn to industries organized around female appearance. Men
with weird hair. Is it wrong of me to bring this up? We do, after
all, move through the world as embodied creatures. I wondered
what it felt like, if you're such a guy, one who's managed to accrue
some significant portion of power in the world—but you're still
you —to coerce sex out of underlings. When you look in the mirror, is it a great white hunter you see staring back, with women
as your game of choice? Sure you've won, you're on top, but isn't
every win a tiny jab of confirmation about your a priori loath-
someness? If sexual domination assuages something for certain
men, is it because somewhere inside lives a puny threatened runt,
and extracting sexual compliance is some form of recompense?
One woman, who'd fought off the advances of a naked, pleading film producer, Harvey Weinstein, recalled that he thereupon
broke into tears and said she'd "rejected him because he was fat."

The mantra lately heard across the land is that sexual harassment isn't about sex, it's about power. I wonder if this under-
thinks the situation: Is the man who won't stop talking about sex

a man convinced of his power, or one who's desperate to impress you with his prowess? Failing to notice the precariousness of power encourages compliance, especially among the women targeted. If recent events tell us anything, it's that power is a *social agreement*, not a stable entity. These despots had power because they did things that were socially valued and profitable, but the terms of the agreement can shift abruptly. (Force is a different thing than power.)

There have been thousands of stories circulating about despicable forms of sexual harassment, and much to process. What's been particularly horrifying to learn is the seriality of the harassment enterprise, the enormous numbers of victims so many of the sexual exploiters racked up. It's like they're on autopilot, programmed to extract sex—or recompense, or humiliation, or something—from unwilling women. Whatever they're after, clearly no quantity of it ever suffices. Learning about other humans acting so robotically presents a conceptual difficulty. We wish to emphasize the moral agency of the predators, their supposed gains—sadistic pleasure, the glee of getting away with it—which enlarges their monstrosity and distinguishes them from the rest of us. But who would "choose" to be a robot?

Some years ago I had coffee with a man who had Tourette's, and whose tic involved touching, which meant that he kept leaning across the small table and touching me on the shoulder, eventually migrating to the breast area. It made me uncomfortable, but I didn't want to mention it because I didn't know if he could control it. Was it lechery or disability?

A similar question nags about some of the sexual malefactors in the news. Former US Congressman Anthony Weiner has been the public face of the sexual tic for some years now: a man of demonstrable intelligence under the sway of a compulsion so intellectually disabling that after a string of previous life-wrecking exposures, he still allowed himself to be set up once again, this time by a fifteen-year-old. Anyone could have seen from ten miles away that it was a frame—anyone but Weiner, that is. (The girl later said she was trying to influence the course of the 2016 presidential election, which she probably did—James Comey, then FBI director, reopened the investigation into Hillary Clinton's e-mails after seizing Weiner's computer once his new friend turned him in.)

Pundits have been quick to pronounce that men such as Weiner aren't sex addicts; they make choices. But neither analysis seems entirely adequate. The question I find myself wanting to ask is: What *happened* to these guys? When you hear of a man masturbating into a potted plant, or behind his desk, or worse, pinning a woman down and masturbating onto her clothes, yes, clearly they hate and need women. Evidently humiliating women is a means to alleviate something. (Psychoanalysts say about flashers that a man's need to whip out and display his penis is to reassure himself that it's still there.) Still, if hatred of women is automatically transmitted to men by a misogynist culture—the customary feminist analysis—why are some men so much more monstrous than others?

One answer, sure to please no one in the condemnation business, was suggested by the feminist Dorothy Dinnerstein's *The Mermaid and the Minotaur* (1976): the problem for men is that they had mothers. Having once been children, a time where women controlled their bodies in humiliating and disempowering ways, men seek to turn the situation around in adulthood. Mother-dominated child-rearing, thought Dinnerstein, is the

reason behind men's loathing of women and everything cultur-
ally inscribed as female. Both men and women remain semi-
human and monstrous under such arrangements, and this is both
our social situation and our personal tragedy: men can't give up
ruling the world until women are finally released from their monopoly on ruling childhood. To push Dinnerstein's speculations
to an even gloomier place, do mothers take out on their sons the
abuses they themselves have suffered at the hands of men? Is this
the result of an understandable frustration at their circumscribed
roles in the world?

Whatever the answer, there's a certain built-in weirdness to
possessing a sexuality, whatever your gender. It reminds us that
we're animals; it's bendable into perverse configurations, which
is maybe what we also like about it. We're afflicted with bizarre,
amoral dreams on a nightly basis. Our fantasy lives don't always
comport with our ideas about who we should be. We go to work
and have to pretend we don't have genitals under our clothes, and
that our coworkers don't either. Maybe this is more of a problem for biological men, given their physiology, which external-
izes desires more blatantly; women are afforded more secrets. But
women can be weirdos and sadists too: the worst fictions about
us are that our natures are pacific and oppression has made us
nobler people. Online feminism is itself a playground of bullying
and viperishness, most of it under the banner of rectitude.

Will men ever see women as full-fledged human beings rather
than ego salves and receptacles? Until that day, the accusations
and exposés will continue: the floodgates have opened and ar-
en't closing anytime soon. That's exciting. No doubt there will
be innocents caught in the crossfire, as distinctions continue to
collapse and mutual suspicion increases (men and women already

resemble red and blue states); as office compliments become af-fronts, and pats on the back actionable.

But it's not exactly news that sexuality fractures self-coher-ence. We're badly held together by social mores and the threat of punishment, which is how we become such good compartmen-talizers. I suspect that anyone who wondered how Harvey Wein-stein could have endowed the Gloria Steinem Chair in Media, Culture and Feminist Studies at Rutgers while serially assault-ing aspiring actresses and assistants is someone who either lacks imagination or has never done a thorough moral inventory.

The "shitty men" revelations were still arriving daily when we started hearing that #MeToo had gone too far, and was now en-croaching on our sexual liberties. These—according to the hun-dred French female signatories of a much-discussed protest letter which ran in *Le Monde*—should include the "right to bother" and the right to "steal" a kiss. Even such benign events as a hand on a knee were being criminalized due to "the hatred of men and sexuality," decried the signatories, one of whom was Catherine Deneuve.

Though this letter struck me as profoundly silly—do men re-ally need more sexual rights than they already have?—I think I understand what's at stake. Certainly for lots of women, espe-cially those of a heterosexual persuasion, being importuned in unpredictable ways—as in men "stealing" kisses—opens up new possibilities; something unexpected and perhaps thrilling has happened. Flirting is where your desirability is confirmed, which is what makes life worth living. Male sexual license can be hot. The worry is that these liminal zones will end up overregulated and boring, that something vital will be lost.

The reason the French counterprotest failed, in my view, is that what's required of us at the moment is being able to hold a dozen contradictory views at once: anything short of this is a failure of imagination. In a situation that demands subtlety, this letter was a sledgehammer. Sure, flirting is fun ... except when it's your gross boss sticking his tongue in your mouth. Sure, stealing kisses is great ... except that it turns women into sexual bounty, not desiring subjects.

When it comes to holding contradictory views, I try to set a useful example. For instance: I've recounted in print more than once posing the question, during a sexual harassment training workshop, "But how do you know an advance is 'unwanted' until you *try*?" Yet I also recently found myself fumingly tweeting, in response to a young female writer's use of the term "predator" to describe a "Powerful Literary Man" who'd once touched her inner thigh in a bar, that the proper term was *asshole*. If I'd wanted self-consistency, I should have given him a pass, right?

No, he was an asshole because his hand was on her inner thigh, which did, arguably, cross a line. The inner thigh is not a liminal zone. There's a reason the "hand on the knee" has become so emblematic in these debates and is such a dividing line in itself: it's because the knee is liminal in a way that, say, the breast is not. A pat on the knee can be sexually benign, but maybe it's not? Everyone knows that if you move a few inches up, all bets are off. Measure the distance from kneecap to crotch, divide it in half, breach that line, and you've entered the zone of the upper thigh—I suspect every woman is aware precisely where that line on her body is, and what trespassing it means. A hand placed above that line requires one to make a decision, in a way that flirting does not. Our bodies are zoned: there are public areas and private ones; parts you can touch without permission, such as my hand, and parts you're trespassing if you encroach on them without my permission.

At the same time, my feeling was that the two were in a bar not at work, and the bar is a liminal zone par excellence. Bars are where we go to drink alcohol, let our inhibitions down, and see what happens. That's the bar's social purpose: to provide a semblance of license in an overregulated world. But how much license is too much license?

Nothing is simple here.

Even though my own #MeToo moments have been largely negligible, and in fact, one of the more memorable of them—which, as it happens, occurred on British soil—actually turned out rather well. I understand the impulse to rain punishment on bodily trespassers. Let me proceed to do so.

The culprit in my case was a future MP and Europe minister, the friend of a friend, which I mention as I understand that MP behavior hasn't always been as stellar as that of elected representatives in my own land. (That was irony.) We were in a group of people heading into a restaurant, and this guy, later to become so politically illustrious, who was walking behind me, and whom I'd met perhaps ten minutes before, reached forward and goosed me. By goosed, I don't mean he touched me *on* my butt, I mean *in* my butt, through my skirt. I turned around and glared at him—I was young, jet-lagged, and confused. Was this customary in Britain? What he'd done felt humiliating. I turned ahead and resolutely kept walking, whereupon he did it again.

When I said things turned out well, what I mean is that he later went to prison. The ostensible reason was for cheating on his expenses, but I like to think it was cosmic justice for his crimes against my person. Inconsequential as they were, untraumatized as I was, I was delighted to see him put away nonetheless, if only for a brief six months. Would Catherine Deneuve say I'm criminalizing the "right to bother"? Perhaps. But why should my body have been enlisted to enlarge his supposed rights, which were clearly plentiful enough? Here was someone perfectly willing to take what wasn't his due in any sphere, and I'm not unhappy to see those latitudes narrowed.

The political necessity of the post-#MeToo moment is insisting that women controlling access to our bodies is the beginning of freedom. Not its terminus, but a starting point. Freedom needs to be more than notional; it also needs to be embodied.

The question for proponents of embodied freedom, and one I've been grappling with myself, is how the #MeToo moment relates to the campus situation I describe in *Unwanted Advances*, which some refer to as "rape culture," about which I used terms like "witch hunt" and "sexual paranoia." The same terminology is now being circulated by #MeToo critics. At first these struck me as very different phenomena. #MeToo is a grassroots movement whose tactics focus on public exposé; in the US, Title IX was imposed by the federal government and administered by campus bureaucrats acting behind closed doors. On campus, the vast majority of accusations are against peers; in #MeToo the setting, at least initially, was largely workplaces and careers. But as #MeToo quickly devolved into complaints about bad sex, awkward come-ons, and offensive jokes, as Human Resource departments stepped in, conducting closed-door investigations and summarily firing those against whom accusations had been made (often without even telling them what they'd been accused of), the situations started looking more and more alike.

What we need, I've begun to think, is a Truth and Reconciliation Commission for bad sex. At the very least we need to be having more tough discussions about nitty-gritty realities of hook-up culture, like the fact that if you're a woman, especially a woman student, having a drunken inexperienced guy on top of you who outweighs you by eighty pounds may not exactly be sexual nirvana. It distresses me to say this some fifty years after the advent of second wave feminism, but real sexual freedom is still a problem for women. For all of us humans, no doubt, but especially for women.

These aren't policy questions alone, they're also existential ones. As far as truth and reconciliation, that would obviously require a lot more truthfulness than we're currently bringing to these discussions. This book was an attempt to put some uncomfortable truths on the table, and see what follows.

April 2018

Introduction:
Sexual Paranoia on Campus

Lately I've been thinking that future generations will look back on the recent upheavals in sexual culture on American campuses and see officially sanctioned hysteria. They'll wonder how supposedly rational people could have succumbed so easily to collective paranoia, just as we look back on previous such outbreaks (Salem, McCarthyism, the Satanic ritual abuse preschool trials of the 1980s) with condescension and bemusement. They'll wonder how the federal government got into the moral panic business, tossing constitutional rights out the window in an ill-conceived effort to protect women students from a rapidly growing catalogue of sexual bogeymen. They'll wonder why anyone would have described any of this as feminism when it's so blatantly paternalistic, or as "political correctness" when sexual paranoia doesn't have any predictable political valence. (Neither does sexual hypocrisy.) Restoring the most fettered versions of traditional femininity through the back door is backlash, not progress.

I didn't exactly mean to stumble into the middle of all this, and I hope that doesn't sound disingenuous. Sure, I like stirring up trouble—as a writer, that is—but believe me, I'm nobody's idea of an activist, quite the reverse. Despite being a left-wing feminist, something in me hates a slogan, even well-intentioned ones like "rape culture." Worse, I tend to be ironic—I *like* irony; it helps you think because it gives you critical distance on a thing. Irony doesn't sit very well in the current climate, especially when it comes to irony *about* the current climate. Critical distance itself is out of fashion—not exactly a plus when it comes to intellectual life (or education itself). Feelings are what's in fashion. I'm all for feelings; I'm a standard-issue female, after all. But this cult of feeling has an authoritarian underbelly: feelings can't be questioned or probed, even while furnishing the rationale for sweeping new policies, which can't be questioned or probed either. (I speak from experience here). The result is that higher education has been so radically transformed that the place is almost unrecognizable.

There are plenty of transformations I'd applaud: more diversity in enrollments and hiring; need-blind admissions; progress toward gender equity. But personally, I dislike being told what I can and can't say. Beyond that, there are pretty important freedoms at stake that are worth fighting to preserve. Hence this book, which I suspect is going to test the limits of what can and can't be said about the sexual and intellectual situation on campus and beyond at the present moment. If this sounds like activism, well, I've been driven to it—entirely *against my own nature*—which shows just how bizarre it's gotten in higher education these days.

When I first heard, in March 2015, that students at the university where I teach had staged a protest march over an essay I'd written about sexual paranoia in academe, and that they were carrying mattresses and pillows, I was a bit nonplussed. For one thing, mattresses had become a symbol of student-on-student sexual assault—a Columbia University student became known as "mattress girl" after spending a year dragging a mattress around campus in a performance art piece meant to protest the university's ruling in a sexual assault complaint she'd filed against a fellow student—whereas I'd been talking about the new consensual relations codes prohibiting professor-student dating. I suppose I knew the essay would be controversial—the whole point of writing it was to say things I believed were true (and suspected a lot of other people thought were true), but weren't being said for fear of repercussions. Still, I'd been writing as a feminist. And I hadn't sexually assaulted anyone. The whole thing seemed incoherent.

According to our student newspaper, the mattress carriers on my campus were marching to the university president's office with a petition demanding "a swift, official condemnation" of my article. One student said she'd had a "very visceral reaction" to it; another called it "terrifying." I'd argued that the new codes infantilized students and ramped up the climate of accusation, while vastly increasing the power of university administrators over all our lives, and here were students demanding to be protected by university higher-ups from the affront of someone's ideas—which seemed to prove my point.

The president announced that he'd consider the petition.

In retrospect, maybe it was shortsighted, but I hadn't actually thought about students reading the essay when I wrote it—who knew students read *The Chronicle of Higher Education*? I'd thought I was writing for other professors and administrators. Despite the petition, I assumed that academic freedom would prevail—for one thing, I'm tenured (thank god), at a research university. Also, I sensed the students weren't going to come off well in the court of public opinion, which proved to be the case. Marching against a published article wasn't a good optic—it smacked of book burning, something Americans generally oppose, while conveniently illustrating my observation in the essay that students' assertions of vulnerability have been getting awfully aggressive in the past few years. Indeed, I was getting a lot of love on social media from all ends of the political spectrum, though one of the anti-PC brigade did email to tell me that, as a leftist, I should realize that these students were my own evil spawn. Yes, I was spending more time online than I should have—though, in fact, social media was my only source of information about the controversy: no one from the university had thought to let me know I was being marched on. (I wasn't teaching that quarter and was trying not to be around much.) I first learned about the events on campus from a journalist in New York.

Let me be the first to admit that being protested has its gratifying side: when the story started getting national coverage, I soon realized my writer friends were all jealous that I'd gotten marched on and they hadn't. I began shamelessly dropping it into conversation whenever possible—"Oh, students are marching against this thing I wrote," I'd grimace, in response to anyone's "How are you?" I briefly fantasized about running for the board of PEN, the international writers' organization devoted to protecting free expression.

Things seemed less amusing when I got an email from the university's Title IX coordinator informing me that two graduate students had filed Title IX complaints against me on the basis of the essay and "subsequent public statements"—this turned out to be a tweet—and that the university had retained a team of outside investigators to handle the case. There were various ominous warnings about keeping the matter confidential.

Perhaps you're wondering how an essay falls under the purview of Title IX, the federal statute meant to address gender discrimination and funding for women's sports? I was wondering that myself, and continued to wonder during the seventy-two-day "investigation" that followed. I'll have plenty more to say about the Title IX process, but the answer, in brief, is that the culture of sexual paranoia I'd been writing about isn't confined to the sexual sphere. It's fundamentally altering the intellectual climate in higher education as a whole, to the point where ideas are construed as threats—writing an essay became "creating a chilling environment," according to my accusers—and freedoms most of us used to take for granted are being whittled away or disappearing altogether. Sexual paranoia has converted the Title IX bureaucracy into an insatiable behemoth, bloated by its own federal power grab, though protests are few because—what are you, in favor of rape culture or something? Also, paranoia is a formula for intellectual rigidity, and its inroads on campus are so effectively dumbing down the place that the traditional ideal of the university—as a refuge for complexity, a setting for the free exchange of ideas—is getting buried under an avalanche of platitudes and fear.

Speaking of dumbing down, and I don't wish to be unkind to either my accusers or my employers, but anyone with half a brain cell could have predicted my response to that Title IX letter in my in-box: an overpowering urge to blow the lid off it all. So shortly later, I wrote a second essay, this one about the Title IX investigation process and my experiences as an accusee (*respondent* is the official term). No professor had previously gone public about a Title IX case, so there was a bit of a tempest—words like *Kafkaesque* and *unconstitutional* got thrown around a lot in the media and online, though it turns out you don't actually have constitutional rights at a private university, which was among the many surprising things I'd come to learn.

That was just the start. It turned out that writing about my case put me on the receiving end of scores of desperate letters and confidential documents relating to *other* people's Title IX cases. It turns out that rampant accusation is the new norm on today's campus; the place is a secret *cornucopia* of accusation, especially when it comes to sex. Including merely *speaking* about sex. My in-box became a clearinghouse for depressing and infuriating tales of overblown charges, capricious verdicts, and frightening bureaucratic excess. I was introduced to an astonishing nether-world of accused professors and students, rigged investigations, closed-door hearings, and Title IX officers run amok. This was a world I'd previously known nothing about, because no one on campus knows anything about it, or no one who hasn't yet been brought up on charges for something. And those in the know are too terrified to speak out because the complaints typically arrive with demands for confidentiality and threats that speaking about the complaints will result in potential job loss or expulsion.

Despite the endless talk about unbridled leftism on campuses, campus political culture of the moment throws all traditional left-right distinctions up for grabs. After I got marched on, I became, for a time, a darling on the right—well, a certain libertarian flange of the right—who liked that I'd stood up to "political correctness," even if I was untrustworthy on every other count. Please note that when someone like me gets lauded on the right, politics as we know it is officially incomprehensible. So let's leave the politics of the campus situation an open question for the moment. Straightforward political explanations are insufficient, and the usual alliances don't hold—we're in the terrain of hysteria, and all bets are off.

Let me attempt to sketch the backdrop of the hysteria, for anyone who hasn't spent time on an American campus lately. There are two conflicting stories about sex at the moment. The first story is all about license: hooking up, binge drinking, porn watching—my students talk knowingly about "anal," and funnily about "dormcest" . . . they're junior libertines, nothing sexual is alien to them.

Layered on top of that is the other big story of the moment: sex is dangerous; it can traumatize you for life.

It's not a happy combination.

For my generation, coming of age in the all-too-brief interregnum after the sexual revolution and before AIDS turned sex into a crime scene replete with perpetrators and victims— back when sex, even when not so great or when people got their feelings hurt, fell under the category of life experience—words like *pleasure* and *liberation* got tossed around a lot. But campus culture has moved on and now the metaphors veer toward the extractive rather than additive—sex takes something *away* from you, at least if you're a woman: your safety, your choices, your future. It's contaminating: you can catch trauma, which, like a virus, never goes away. You don't hear much talk about liberation anymore; the slogans are all about sexual assault and other encroachments: "Stop Rape Culture," "No Means No," "Control Yourselves, Not Women."

Sexual assault *is* a reality on campus, though not exactly a new one. But despite all the recent attention and the endless flurry of statistics, it's still an incredibly underexamined reality, permeated by speech taboos and barbed-wire fences meant to deter intellectual intruders. We're never going to decrease sexual assault on campus—a goal I assume everyone shares—if we can't have open conversations about it. Having control over your body is, especially for women, a learned skill; it requires education. It also requires a lot more honesty about the complicated sexual realities hiding behind the slogans than is currently permissible. My question becomes: what contradictions are we not supposed to notice, hiding in plain sight behind those large No Trespassing signs?

Let me venture a few possibilities. To begin with, the endangerment story produces huge blind spots, which are reproduced in every new policy and code supposedly meant to reduce unwanted sex. The policies are ineffectual because the endangerment story and the realities of sexual assault are two entirely separate things. That's blind spot number one. About those realities: the underlying gender dynamic is blind spot number two—the dynamic between men and women, I mean. Men *and* women. What I'm saying is that policies and codes that bolster traditional femininity—which has always favored stories about female endangerment over stories about female agency—are the *last* thing in the world that's going to reduce sexual assault, which is the argument at the heart of this book.*

---

* The issues are predominantly male-female, though same-sex relationships can be subject to the same forces—in fact, a case between two male students (*Doe v. Brandeis*) may affect how many other future student cases are adjudicated. Doe, a male student, was found guilty of sexual

Whether or not college students are actually *having* sex any differently from generations past, clearly the emphasis has changed. Shifting the stress from pleasure to danger and vulnerability not only changes the prevailing narrative, it changes the way sex is experienced. We're social creatures, after all, and narrative is how we make sense of the world. If the prevailing story is that sex is dangerous, sex is going to feel threatening more of the time, and anything associated with sex, no matter how innocuous (a risqué remark, a dumb joke) will feel threatening.

Teaching under these conditions can feel like a tightrope walk. A few years ago, I was having a conversation with a class about a movie—*The Opposite of Sex*, fittingly enough. I teach film. A student (female) made a comment assailing the female lead's poor sexual choices, pronouncing, a bit Cotton Mather-ishly, upon the character's irresponsibility and sexual risk-taking, a judgment with which most of the class concurred. My students are all writing screenplays and making films, and the consensus startled me: first, because I spend a lot of energy trying to *get* students to understand that moralizing about characters isn't a great way to go about writing interesting ones—characters aren't *supposed* to be

---

misconduct after his boyfriend of nearly two years, "J.C.," charged (six months after their breakup) that numerous instances of sex during their relationship had been nonconsensual. Brandeis's "special examiner" found Doe guilty of "violence" toward J.C.—effectively conflating violence with "virtually any form of unwanted sexual activity," said a federal judge in allowing the case to proceed. The examiner even found that John's kissing J.C. while he was asleep constituted sexual misconduct, because a person who's sleeping can't give consent. The judge used the term *logical fallacies* about such conclusions, though they're par for the course in campus adjudications these days.

upstanding citizens—and second, because we all knew that some percentage of the class (or their peer group, anyway) was making similar sexual choices not infrequently, which is why Plan B birth control is available on demand at the student health service.

I know this because I probably get to know my students better than a lot of professors do. One reason is that they're frequently pillaging their own lives for material. Often at the end of the quarter, a student volunteers the information that a script or film was autobiographical, though I generally don't ask. My teaching method, such as it is, mostly involves talking about movies and hashing over students' creative ideas with them, so they're doing a majority of the talking, and I'm hearing what they think about love, sex, morality, and so on. I wouldn't claim to be the world's greatest teacher, but there are students who like my approach (some do, some don't) and who take multiple classes with me; these kids I get to know especially well. It puts me in a fairly good position to compare the mind-set of at least this subsection of the student population with mine at their age, and the differences in attitude continually startle me, especially when it comes to the propensity for moralizing.

My own education was in art schools, where the pedagogical style was admittedly pretty casual. The teachers who influenced me the most were gnomic oddballs. Some of them were brutal—I recall one guy, a painter, yelling "This is shit!" during a critique, though thankfully not at me. I also recall drunken parties at his loft—students and teachers getting plastered together was a regular event. You didn't feel your teachers were remote, all-powerful beings—they were messy, opinionated, depressed, monumentally flawed. We took them seriously because of their ideas, not their institutional roles. *Safety*, the watchword of the contemporary campus, would have been a term of derision for us, reserved for a painting that matched the sofa.

I recall another teacher, a Marxist-Freudian bodybuilder who I'm pretty sure never published anything and was reputedly sleeping his way through a swathe of the student population, who influenced me more than any teacher before or since. The ideas I first encountered in his Modern Art History class shaped the entirety of my intellectual repertoire. One day I got up my nerve and asked him out; he said no. I was mortified, but managed to gather what small shred of self-regard remained and keep going to class. I wrote a wildly speculative final paper he praised effusively, one that contained arguments I'm still working out to this day.

Among the many things wrong with the sex-as-danger preoccupation on campuses now—and here I'm speaking as someone teaching on the creative side of the curriculum—is that zealous boundary-drawing and self-protective preciousness don't augur well for the imaginative life. Can creativity be taught? Probably not, though I do think you can encourage the conditions that improve its chances, and defensiveness isn't one of those conditions. But I don't preach about such things to my students; I generally just try to figure out what they're struggling to say and help them push it further. At most, I confine myself to pointing out (tactfully, I hope) when I think they're coasting on clichés.

My class's moralizing about the poor sexual choices in *The Opposite of Sex* seemed to be such an occasion. Moralizing isn't thinking; it comes too easily, it's too smug (especially coming from moralizing libertines). I'd wanted them to see how the surprise pregnancy motored the plot, rather than just denounce the character. After they were done trashing her, I said, attempting to offer another angle, "Gosh, I feel sorry for you guys. When I was in school we thought about sex in terms of pleasure; your generation seems to think about it all in terms of risk."

Another student (male) exclaimed, "Well, yeah, sex can kill you!"

I've thought about that remark a lot since then. It was a great lesson in the obvious: which is that this generation of students, millennials, is also the first post-AIDS generation. God knows what horrors they've been exposed to in their Sex Ed classes—necessarily, I suppose, but still, with what effects? Not vastly increased levels of self-acuity, and though we're all stragglers when it comes to sexual honesty, I suspect, from what I've observed, that this generation has it far worse (possibly contributing to the stratospheric levels of binge drinking, which we'll be getting to—who wouldn't want to shed a few layers of doomsaying on the weekends?).

Obviously there's nothing new about a youthful education in the hazards of sex—I recall disgusting slide shows of syphilitic sex organs in my own junior high Sex Ed class—as each aging generation is all too pleased to educate the next one in the standard perils: pregnancy, disease, shame, spiritual corruption, and so on. The danger of sex may be a recurring cultural script, but what's still worth pointing out is how it shapes gender roles, and colors how gender is lived, especially for women. Women are situated differently from men when it comes to sexual danger (though, according to social science research, we typically also *feel* ourselves to be far more vulnerable to sexual danger than we are—and I can think of no better way to subjugate women than to convince us that assault is around every corner). Still, for my generation of women, there was hardly the same death knell tolling in the background.

For us, post-Pill and after second-wave feminism had made at least a few provisional inroads into female shame and the double standard, sex wasn't exactly uncomplicated, but even when it was bad (as it often was), it was still educational. Even today's cardinal danger, sex with teachers, which many of us dabbled in without too many horrible consequences, was educational. A high percentage of the women I know have a teacher or two in their past; most, as far as I can tell, regard these experiences fondly. Or, even when feelings are mixed, it wasn't some sort of awful trauma. When I look back on it now, I wonder who I'd have become without all the bad sex, the flawed teachers, and the liberty to make mistakes. I got to take risks, which was a training ground for later creative and intellectual risks, precisely because we didn't *think* of sex as a harm.

Just to be clear, I'm not trying to say that my generation's story about pleasure was any *truer* than this one's story about danger. There's no singularly true way of thinking about sex and no direct way of experiencing it: how we think about sex is always going to be filtered through whatever shifting set of cultural suppositions prevails. Call this "sexual ideology" or "sexual culture," but there aren't fixed truths about sex, or reliable facts. All we have are fluctuating emotional colors and tendencies presenting themselves in the guise of truths and facts. And no matter how many statistics and percentages get thrown around to buttress the fantasy that there's some "objective" way of knowing the truth of sex, nothing's more unreliable than sexual statistics—humans are horrendous at sexual self-reporting, to begin with. Everyone lies about sex, though maybe every generation lies about sex differently, or so I've been thinking of late. All we can say is that the "truth" of sex has been different at every point in history, that every era believes its own sexual narrative to be the truth of sex, and at this point the dominant narrative, on the nation's campuses anyway, is all about *hazard.*

The problem is that this shift in sexual culture isn't confined to sex; it's more like a land grab, gobbling up vast swathes of real estate along the way, including the very definition of what it is to be a woman. When it comes to sexual culture, obviously each generation bills itself as an improvement over the last. No doubt the slogans about pleasure and liberation were our little lies about sex—the realities were obviously a lot thornier, especially for women. But today's hazard story, too, comes with its own evasions, namely the blind spot about women's agency. In a sexual culture that emphasizes female violation, endangerment, and perpetual vulnerability ("rape culture"), men's power is taken as a given instead of interrogated: men need to be policed, women need to be protected. If rape is the norm, then male sexuality is by definition predatory; women are, by definition, prey. Regulators thus rush in like rescuing heroes, doing what it takes to fend off the villains—*whatever* it takes, since when women are imperiled, vigilantism is the better part of heroism. At least, that's the tradition, a tradition with a lot of racial baggage in the American context, it's worth mentioning—in fact a founding American myth. (See John Ford's *The Searchers,* with John Wayne exemplifying just how psychosexually convoluted the whole rescuing-women enterprise can be.)

And here's where I say, as a feminist: this is terrible for women. We *all,* men and women both, want the law to protect us from unequal strength and exercises of violence: the brute can't be allowed to rule because he's larger or stronger. The law bridges the gap in bodily differences to provide equity between citizens. But why treat sexual assault as the paradigmatic female experience when there are plenty of other female experiences in which women's embodied, physiological differences from men materially impede gender equity? As a feminist, I want to see the government step in to remedy those, too. I don't mean just pay equity, the conventional demand. I mean making child care and maternity costs free, which would obviously be the fastest path to real equity for the greatest number of women. This is an issue you hear pretty much zero about on American campuses these days, by the way. Instead, all historical inequities between the genders have been relocated to the sexual sphere and displaced onto sexual danger, with paranoia substituting for sustained thought or historical perspective.

When I say "substituting for sustained thought," here's an example. I spoke with a young man I'll call Simon, until recently a student at a Big Ten university, who, following a brief closed-door hearing, was "excluded" for two years (expelled, effectively) for the use of "emotional and verbal coercion" in a sexual situation involving his then girlfriend and an ambivalent blow job on her part. Emotional and verbal coercion means that he asked her for a blow job, and she complied, after first demurring. There was no finding of physical force. He was eighteen at the time, a freshman. The girlfriend was a year older. He said she verbally assented; she said she didn't.* When he realized she wasn't into it,

---

* I'm reporting the accuser's side of the story based on the university's report (I had access to a redacted version). I didn't interview the accuser in this case or the other cases I discuss, which would have been impossible—any respondent who gave me the name or contact information for a complainant would be subject to retaliation charges. The privacy constraints are one thing

he halted things, he says, after thirty seconds or so. He thought he was being flirtatious when he'd asked for oral sex, he told me with embarrassment—this was not someone brimming with sexual confidence. There had been previous sex between the two, and previous blow jobs; the charge of coercion came months later, following a breakup.

The ruling was that he should have known that consent had to be "voluntary, present and ongoing." For campus officials to find this kid responsible for "emotional coercion" not only means prosecuting students for the awkwardness of college sex, it also brands an eighteen-year-old a lifelong sex criminal—all college applications now ask if a student has been found responsible for "behavioral misconduct" at a previous institution, and demand the details. He assumes he'll never get into another school and is adamant he'll never return to the previous one, even if he could. His life is wrecked, he feels.

If incidents like these are being labeled sexual assault, then we need far more discussion about just how capacious this category is becoming, and why it's in anyone's interests. Including women's. What a lot of retrogressive assumptions about gender are being promulgated under the guise of combating assault! Not only was the woman's agency erased, note the unarticulated premise of the finding: women students aren't men's equals in *emotional* strength or self-possession, and require teams of campus administrators to step in and remedy the gap. Another

---

that make Title IX difficult to write about (also so impervious to oversight). Those interested in reading more from the point of view of accusers might consult Annie E. Clark and Andrea L. Pino's *We Believe You: Survivors of Campus Sexual Assault Speak Out* (Holt, 2016).

unarticulated premise: sex is injurious and the woman had sustained an injury in that thirty seconds, one serious enough to require official remediation. My question: how much are such unexamined premises contributing to the ballooning number of sexual allegations, and to women's own self-identification as perpetually injured parties?

None of this is to diminish the reality of sexual assault. At the same time, we seem to be breeding a generation of students, mostly female students, deploying Title IX to remedy sexual ambivalences or awkward sexual experiences, and to adjudicate relationship disputes post-breakup—and campus administrators are allowing it. If this is what feminism on campus has come to, then seriously, let's just cash it in and start over, because this feminism is broken. It has exactly nothing to do with gender equity or emancipating women—a cynic might say it actually has more to do with extending the reach of campus bureaucracy into everyone's lives. It's a vast, unprecedented transfer of power into the hands of the institution. But whatever the agenda, and whoever the secret beneficiaries, hard-fought rights, namely the right for women to be treated as consenting adults in erotic matters, are being handed back on a platter.

The problem, of course, is that it's also all far messier than this. There are plenty of cases where unequivocal sexual assaults happen and the system fails to deal with it—especially when it comes to athletes and frats—even as there are shocking prosecutorial excesses in other instances. There's no coherence to the situation. But weaponizing Title IX isn't going to fix the sexual assault problem. If anything's going to make a dent, it's education, and the educational system is failing to educate anyone, largely because speaking honestly about sexual realities has become taboo.

Speaking of realities: a few additional thoughts on the term *rape culture* and why I can't sign on. The idea of rape culture has become the campus equivalent of 9/11: in both cases, horrible real events take on mythic proportions, becoming resistant to precise analysis. On campus, the term *rape culture*, like the term *terrorism*, has become the rhetoric of emergency. Fear becomes the guideline, promulgating more fear. The problem is that fear rhetoric obfuscates more than it explicates; nevertheless, official-dom leaps to action. Hawks demand an over-response, such as going to war on false pretenses. The failed war exacerbates the fears, which becomes the rationale for further expanding the security state: vast expenditures, increased layers of bureaucracy, surveillance, secret renditions, summary justice—like expelling a freshman for "emotional coercion."

The term *carceral feminism* has been used to describe the hawkish security state swerve in social policy on women's issues: more policing (*carceral* derives from *incarceration*), more regulation, an eagerness to trade away civil liberties for illusory promises of safety, and the same complacent failures of analysis. Carceral feminism—the term was invented by Barnard sociologist Elizabeth Bernstein—is pretty much the guiding spirit in campus policy, and it's a profoundly conservative, law-and-order spirit, with resources diverted away from education and toward punishment. Even if no one's going around wearing little flag lapel pins, the idea that this is some kind of left-wing plot strikes me as short on . . . intelligence.

It's long been true of mainstream American feminism that the most supposedly radical factions have been closet conservatives, dedicated to recycling the most conventional versions of feminine virtue and delicacy. There have always been puritanical versions of feminism competing with more emancipatory versions. The so-called radical feminists of the 1980s—the designation was always a misnomer—were short-sighted bluenoses, even aligning themselves with Christian conservatives to fight the demon pornography (just as some first-wave feminists joined with prohibitionists to fight the demon rum). Breaking with the radicals, "liberal feminists" were the faction focused on pay equity and workplace issues. The problem was that having also broken with the male-dominated New Left (not without good reason: they tended to be jerks to women), class and race mostly dropped out of the discussion. While European feminists with a social democratic tradition behind them were demanding and getting subsidized day care, winning resources from the state and employers, their American liberal counterparts favored "networking" (more recently, "leaning in"). The new goal: breaking into the ranks of corporate CEOs. Result: every American mother still has to figure out for herself what to do with the kids while she's at work, since given the new winner-take-all economy, it takes two or more jobs to support a family.

Meanwhile, a new generation of student activists, legitimately dissatisfied with the legacies of liberal feminism, rather than looking to revitalize the socialist or left-emancipatory traditions, are instead joining arms with campus administrators as the fast track to empowerment. But even if the rhetoric borrows from radicalism, the substance is far from it. Ah, look: there's the familiar anti-porn keenness for female captivity narratives in an updated guise. Sure, the updated version nixes the anti-porn agenda per se, which would seem old-fashioned—even suburban housewives these days claim to love porn—though the shopworn tale of women held hostage by male sexual impulses still gets a lot of play.

How is it that the most reactionary versions of feminism are the ones enjoying the greatest success on campuses? For one thing, those are the versions reaping the institutional support, not least in Washington. Perhaps there's also something reassuringly familiar—at least timeless—about these tales of female peril, even amidst the supposed sexual free-for-all of hookup culture.

So all this was in the back of my mind when the *Chronicle* asked me to write an essay on campus sexual politics. Mulling it over, I recalled the notice that had arrived by email a year or so before (out of the blue, it seemed), banning all dating, romantic, or sexual relations between undergraduates and faculty members, consensual or not. Relationships between faculty and grad students were described as "problematic" and though not outright prohibited, had to be disclosed to your department chair, if and when such a relationship commenced.

I'd felt a surge of annoyance on receipt of this email, not that I especially wanted to date students. There were already harassment codes on the books prohibiting nonconsensual relations or contact, so why prohibit consensual activity? It struck me as antifeminist, yet another puncture to female autonomy—even though the language was gender-neutral, I was pretty sure it was women these codes meant to protect, including from their own desires and ambivalences.

Before the email's arrival, students and professors could romance whomever we wished; the next day we were off-limits to

one another—verboten, traife, dangerous . . . though perhaps
therefore all the more alluring? (Not something the regulators
seem to have considered.) It all seemed massively hypocritical,
given the legions of professors who've dated a student or two in
their day. More than a few female professors, too; in fact, I'm one
of them. Don't ask for details—it's one of those things it now
behooves one to be reticent about, lest you be branded a sex fiend.

And what about the legions of professors actually *married* to
their former students, including a few in my own department?
I mean, you can barely throw a stone on most campuses around
the country without hitting a few dozen examples. I confess I
felt a little sorry for them all: once respectable citizens, lead-
ers in their fields, department chairs, deans, more than a few
college presidents, transformed by the new regulatory zeal into
abusers of power *avant la lettre*, even though professor-student
romances were once practically an educational norm. And think
how their kids must feel! A friend of mine is the offspring of such
a coupling—does she look at her parents a little differently now?

Needless to say, these are not questions being pondered on
campus, since the subject can't be openly spoken of. I noticed none
of these "mixed" couples were coming forward to speak out against
the new codes, by the way, putting this newly outlawed sexual
minority more or less where gays were pre-Stonewall. Student-
teacher relationships: the love that dare not speak its name.

I suppose it's a universal thing about sex (as I think anthropologists have variously observed) that it requires prohibitions, even
if the particulars of what's permitted and prohibited keep shifting around. As we see on campus: on the one hand, all sorts of
practices and identities not so long ago regarded as outré (trans-
genderism, polyamory, BDSM, and queerness of every stripe) are

newly ascendant, whereas practices that were not so long ago the norm (professor-student dating) have suddenly been recoded as criminal enterprises. Along with awkward sex, ambivalent sex— even the wrong eye contact can get you brought up on complaints at present. I recently heard about a male grad student filing a Title IX complaint against a female professor for dancing "too provocatively" at an off-campus party. All of which is worth some intellectual analysis, an activity you used to encounter with regularity on campuses. In lieu of analysis, we get sweeping regulations and faculty silence. Maybe there are isolated pockets of opposition, but for the most part dissenters are keeping a low profile, like skeptics during the Inquisition.

Another of the weirder features of campus life now is witnessing a generation of students demanding *more* regulation over their lives from the administration, in contrast to the demands of previous generations of activists that campus officials get *out* of their lives. Our rebellions were more straightforwardly Oedipal: overthrow everything, especially the fucking administration. (Watergate was still a cultural landmark.) In my own first semester of college long ago, students staged a protest to oust the college president, who was regarded as a venal megalomaniac; after a no-support vote by the faculty shortly later, he handed in his resignation. *That's* how you deal with overreaching administrators, I'd always assumed. Of course, today's college students are also the generation known to be best friends with their parents, as many of my own students are, chatting with them multiple times a day, as far as I can tell ("Love you, Mom, talk later" one frequently hears students chirping into their cells as they rush into class), so maybe they regard administrators with more benevolence than my era did.

The fiction of benevolent officialdom requires a certain historical amnesia, particularly when it comes to sexual minorities. Not long ago a gay male professor wrote to tell me he'd been accused by a former advisee, also male—there'd been a falling out between them—of groping a female grad student at a party. The professor testified at his Title IX hearing that he hadn't touched a woman sexually in thirty-two years, but the entirety of his sexuality (and every other foible, along with his teaching—had there been risqué remarks in the classroom?) was now under the institutional microscope; he was eventually fired. I couldn't help reflecting that this was unfolding around the same time that movie audiences were weeping piously over the story of the hounded gay mathematician Alan Turing in *The Imitation Game* (who committed suicide after being subjected to chemical castration to "treat" his homosexuality), while oblivious to the houndings playing out on our nation's campuses.

The history of sexual outlawry is one reason it's dispiriting to find student activists, all assiduously pro-sex and genderqueer (at least sporting a lot of piercings and other insignias of nonconformity), joining arms with campus bureaucrats to demand wider prosecutorial nets for professorial sex offenders. Apparently no one has mentioned to them how many of the professors being caught in these widening nets are, in fact, queer—or suspected of being so, anyway. A woman professor I met while visiting another campus revealed she'd been brought up on Title IX complaints for making "suspicious eye contact" with two female graduate students, staring at one's chest, and whispering in their ears. It so happened that the whispering took place in a library; her field was library science. She told the story in a funnily bitter way, but it was probably not so funny at the time. She was summoned to a three-hour meeting, not told what the charges were or who had complained, and then not allowed to set foot on campus for two months while the case was in progress. In other words, she was treated like a sex offender ordered to stay away from playgrounds. Perhaps you're thinking she was one of those lesbian predators who prowl academe in search of luscious young prey? Perhaps her students were thinking so, too—she does have short hair and an authoritative bearing, but is as straight as they come, at least according to her. (I didn't ask, she volunteered the information.)

One centrally placed queer theorist of my acquaintance, always in the know when it comes to professional gossip, tells me that more gay and queer than straight professors are the subject of formal complaints. Who knows? It's not as though we have data on any of this, since it all takes place in secret. Her point was that gay and queer professors invariably become targets of projection for sexually confused students, though from what I've been learning, no particular group has a monopoly on sexual confusion.

Terms such as *coddled* have been thrown around a lot lately about this generation of students, and it's true that officialdom is abundantly *there* for students (especially at pricier places), though why shouldn't they get concierge service given the rising price of tuition? Of course a large reason tuition costs are climbing is the growth of officialdom. The ratio of administrators to students has nearly doubled since 1975, political scientist Benjamin Ginsberg reports in *The Fall of the Faculty: The Rise of the All-Administrative University and Why It Matters*, while the ratio of faculty to students has stayed constant. These administrative hires often have no academic background, yet they're the ones making policies and setting the tenor of the place. They're also typically paid a lot more than faculty.

When the students gathered to protest my essay, three administrators (the dean of students, the director of student conduct and conflict resolution, and the coordinator of sexual violence response services) joined the group and, according to the campus newspaper, lauded the students for taking a stand. When I was in school—yes, I know the phrase makes me sound like a geezer—the old people in charge of things weren't in cahoots with our sexual narrative, which at least provided something bracing to rebel against: an antithesis, some contestation. Now old people and young ones (at least the more vocal among the young) all seem to share the same proprieties.

It does make me grateful to have been educated in a time when the holders of institutional power weren't regarded as quite so benign. Nor were the institutions themselves so mollifying, so ambitious about fixing our lives. I wonder if being in school now would have left me feeling less freedom to act on the world, perhaps more beholden to authority? I feel a touch of regret on behalf of my students, the women especially, whose freedoms have become so much more straitened, in proportion to the fears and assuagements of the times.

Though even saying this puts me out of step with campus verities. In the student-as-consumer model, we're frequently urged to see the world from a student-eye point of view, to substitute their wisdom for our own. High on the activist-administrator joint agenda is reeducating the professoriate to be more sensitive to students' feelings, which includes their feelings of disempowerment vis-à-vis us, their professors. Especially in need of reeducation are the older campus fogeys—tenured white guys are mostly in the crosshairs—and a few others deemed not with the program, which I guess would include me, as someone who has to suppress eye-rolling fits at the obligatory platitudes.

Had you been there to witness my reaction to a recent memo sent to the faculty in my department by one of our undergrad majors, imploring us to "be conscious of the vocabulary and discourse used in your classroom" and to "challenge ideas of gender, rape culture, whiteness and heteronormativity" in the teaching of our classes, you'd understand what I mean. Why does the purgatory of the nice place have to entail so many empty slogans? I fumed silently. There I was, huffing and puffing like some bow-tied neocon: this isn't intellect, I snorted (to myself); it's virtue-mongering. And yet: did I send a prickly reply pointing out to my young correspondent that all these terms have tangled and contested histories and meanings, that good intentions are fine, but we're all still supposed to be thinking for ourselves? I did not, because I'm fairly sure that if I had, I'd have been creating "a hostile learning environment," and I'm fairly certain there are codes against that.

Sure, there have always been ideologues on campuses, but the old ideologues were at least expected to argue the validity of their ideas. The new brand are ideologues of feelings, and feelings can't be argued. Despite being a certified left-wing feminist, I just don't believe that experience or identity credentialize you intellectually. In fact, it's usually the opposite: overvaluing subjectivity has a way of stunting intellectual growth, especially when it comes to ideas that threaten your self-coherence, which the best ideas often do. The latest demands for intellectual conformity may come in progressive packaging, but feminists and leftists should be flinging these pieties away like lumps of dung, not kowtowing to the virtue parade.

The irony about this insistence on student vulnerability is how successful it's been as a tactic for accruing administrative power. Encouraging students' sense of fragility is swelling the ranks of potentially jobless professors while bolstering the power of administrations over faculty. As more of us get charged with newly invented crimes, more administrators get hired to adjudicate them, administrators whose powers blossom the more malfeasance they can invent to ferret out. Which means that in a situation already prone to projection and fantasy—teaching—faculty are sitting ducks for accusations made by emotionally troubled students (and the onset age for such troubles is often late adolescence and early twenties), for whom we're likely to become parental proxies and love/hate legatees. But what do Title IX officers care about projection?

Sexuality is a complicated business. Emotional distress comes with the territory some percentage of the time. There's a remarkable episode in Elena Ferrante's Neapolitan novels, where Elena, the narrator, decides to lose her virginity to Donato Sarratore, the father of the boy she's in love with. She's sixteen or seventeen at the time, and on the one hand, Donato disgusts her—his flowery language ("sleazy lyricizing"), his advanced age. Yet she's weirdly sexually compelled by him. She likes how he makes her feel. She wants to feel like a different person: he's her transit to a new self. After they have sex she reflects that she has no regrets, then coldly dumps him. Later she'll look back on the episode with more mixed feelings, but in the moment, it feels empowering.

One of the attractions of fiction is that fictional characters open themselves to contradictory desires better than we readers do. But I wonder whether any of my students, schooled in the simplistic catechisms of the moment, will end up capable of as much ferocious emotional complexity in their work as a novelist like Ferrante manages to achieve. As a teacher, I do what I can to get them to think about their responses to the world as questions, not givens; to forestall the easy moralizing. When I really want to cause my supposedly sexually with-it students a world of despair, I like to bring up Freud. "If we didn't desire to have sex with our parents or vice versa, why would we need a taboo?" I've been known to inquire innocently when a discussion turns to, say, family dynamics, or they tell me Freud is passé. Their faces fall; there are audible cries of alarm and disgust. "Doesn't everyone dream about having sex with their parents once in a while?" I once asked, trying to explain the Freudian concept of dreams as a playground for repressed wishes—I nearly got ejected from my own classroom. Without repression, what would stop us from going around having sex with anyone in sight, including our siblings and maybe the family dog? I go on. More cries of disgust from the class. (I'm not claiming that such discussions make me popular.) I'm just trying to introduce them to the idea that we're all constituted by taboos and repressions we're not entirely aware of: that's the human situation. Disgust is what repression looks like. The unruliness of sexual desire has always required a certain level of prohibition, not to mention dissembling. Say hello to the incest taboo, the founding gesture of social organization, say anthropologists. Where would we be without it? In bed with our parents, that's where. Ugh. Perhaps such ideas are especially threatening for a generation whose closeness to their parents is already so intimate—I've sometimes wondered about the role of over-parenting in campus sexual politics. You hear a lot of accusations about helicopter parents as regards the supposedly coddled kids—the right especially loves this line of attack—but I mean something deeper. Namely: why *is* intergenerational sex such a great taboo at this moment, when not so long ago it was no big thing? (If you want evidence, look at all those professor-student marriages.) What's shifted?

Freud is also a handy figure when it comes to the connections between desire and prohibition. Freud's general surmise, as everyone knows, was that children desire their parents, same-sex parent as well as opposite. (Recall that Freud thought everyone starts out bisexual.) This desire undergoes social repression; neurosis results. Of course it's an article of faith at the moment that all such desires run strictly in the other direction: old people desire young ones, not the other way around.

Please understand that I'm not encouraging anyone to sleep with their parents (or their teachers). I don't care if my students buy the Freudian line (it's a heuristic, not a set of unassailable truths)—I only care that they're thinking in creative ways. Where Freud becomes useful, especially for my students, aspiring writers and directors (or for anyone interested in plumbing psychological depths), is as the patron saint of failed self-awareness, the great disrupter of self-certainty—especially if you take seriously the various dispatches from the Freudian annals about how little we actually know ourselves, particularly when it comes to attractions and repulsions. If I can get a student to look at herself as a mystery, a bundle of mixed motives and ambivalences, I know for a fact the chances are better she'll produce some original work. Does this make my classroom an "unsafe space?" I hope so, obviously, though I'm going to (mostly) refrain from mocking students for demanding "safe spaces," which I consider low-hanging fruit.

The problem is this: the more that "safety" means lowering the bar for accusation-bringing, then the more of a magnet the process becomes, and *has* become, for anyone with an agenda, a grudge, a neurosis, and sometimes financial ambitions—payouts can be huge for a well-timed claim—and there's no adequate method for sorting legitimate from specious claims (as we'll see). It's not in administrators' interests *to* sort them: a campus's success in "combatting sexual assault" is measured in increased accusations, which are closely tracked. By the way, complaints can increasingly be made *anonymously*—which is to say that witch hunt conditions are now an institutionalized feature of campus life.

Speaking of witches: the ostensible grounds for the Title IX complaints against me were that I'd written a few paragraphs in "Sexual Paranoia Strikes Academe" (maybe four) about one of these supposed witches. This was a disgraced philosophy professor on our campus named Peter Ludlow, who'd been accused twice of sexual misconduct. I suspected that the case against him arose largely from the new campus paranoia, and alluded to that possibility in the essay.

Ludlow and I had never met—everything I wrote was based on publicly available information—though our lives would become weirdly intertwined, due, largely, to the shortsightedness of zealotry.

One valuable lesson I've learned from my recent experiences, and one I'd wish to convey to all aspiring brimstoners and code wielders, is that zealotry can boomerang in unanticipated ways. Because my accusers overplayed their hand by trying to bend Title IX into an all-purpose bludgeon (enabled by campus officials, it must be said, though they have their own overseers of course: the feds), Ludlow and I did eventually meet, and the more I learned about his situation, the more I saw his case as a lens through which the excesses and hypocrisies of the current campus hysteria came into focus.

A year or so after I'd first written those four paragraphs in *The Chronicle*, I flew down to Mexico to interview him for this book. This was February 2016. He'd moved there because he could live cheaply—he'd pretty much lost everything by that point. He'd resigned his position, and his employment prospects were nonexistent. The publicity about the charges against him had been intense. Before the accusations, there'd been a big job offer from one of the best philosophy departments in the country (Rutgers), which he'd accepted; the offer was withdrawn after students there got word about student protests against him on our campus and staged protests of their own. Once at the top of his field, Ludlow was now such a professional pariah that two book contracts were cancelled and other philosophers wouldn't even publish articles in the same volume with him. He'd been effectively blacklisted.

No doubt there are people who'd say he had it coming—he "wasn't a eunuch," in his own words—though I tend to think that's like saying John Proctor in *The Crucible* had it coming. The reference is to Arthur Miller's play about the Salem witch trials. (Proctor was one of the accused witches, hanged by the community.) Seen as a parable of McCarthyism when it was first staged in 1953, the play was recently revived on Broadway—apparently someone saw it as relevant again. The Cold War blacklist, too, is being plumbed for current resonances. A recent biopic about Hollywood Ten screenwriter Dalton Trumbo (forced out of work and imprisoned after falling afoul of the House Un-American Activities Committee's witch hunt investigation of communism in the movie industry) left me reflecting that sex is our era's Communist threat, and Title IX hearings our new HUAC hearings. Except this time around, they're under the direction of the Department of Education, not Congress.

One consequence of resigning was that Ludlow left the university without a confidentiality agreement: unlike other accused professors and students, he could talk about his case with anyone he wanted. At one point, there had been a settlement offer on the table; no doubt it would have contained the usual confidentiality clause. It was withdrawn after students got word and marched against any settlement, which is where the shortsightedness of zealotry comes in.

Ludlow's parting wave—he had nothing to lose by that point—was bestowing on me the files from his investigation: the Title IX reports and thousands of pages of background material. (Bureaucracies produce a lot of paper.) It's an unprecedented behind-the-scenes view of just how haphazard and, frankly, incompetent the Title IX process can be. Reading it was incredibly eye-opening—in fact, a lot of what I read was shocking, and I'm not exactly unjaded when it comes to institutional power.

The reason I'm relating Ludlow's story in the pages to come isn't because it happened on my campus, or because my campus is worse than others when it comes to sanctioning witch hunts. It's because a trove of documents landed in my lap, and the story they tell should see the light of day exactly because this *isn't* just Ludlow's story. From what I've learned in the last year and a half, these sorts of arbitrary and often outlandish tribunals are being conducted at colleges and universities all over the country, with accused faculty and students being stripped of their rights and, in many instances, simply hung out to dry to give the appearance that higher ed is mobilized against sexual assault.

The reality is that a set of incomprehensible directives, issued by a branch of the federal government, are being wielded in wildly idiosyncratic ways, according to the whims and biases of individual Title IX officers operating with no public scrutiny or accountability. Some of them are also all too willing to tread on academic and creative freedom as they see fit. Not long ago I spoke to a creative writing teacher who'd been grilled by his campus's Title IX officer about why he'd taught poems with sexual content in a writing workshop. I also read the lengthy self-defense he prepared, which included a defense not just of his teaching methods, but of Walt Whitman, a previous era's sexual renegade and, according to many, America's greatest poet. (Whitman had come up in the investigation; it wasn't clear if the investigators knew of him.)

Not to sound like a doom-monger, but this is the face of something gone incredibly wrong in higher education.

Writing this book has forced me to realize something about myself, or maybe a couple of things. The first is how disillusioned I've become, in the last few years, about the state of intellectual honesty on American campuses. Campus life has gotten so ludicrous and censorious that it hardly seems worth caring. It's far more impossible to have an intellectually honest discussion about sex on campus *on* an American campus than off these days, which is nothing short of bizarre if you're someone who was drawn to academia in the first place because talking about difficult stuff was supposedly what went on there.

The second thing I realized is that if I could get this disillusioned, I was probably more invested in the place than I'd thought.

Despite my laments about higher ed and its current afflictions, someone once referred to being a professor as the last good job in America, and with that I completely concur. I'm lucky to be employed by my university (despite our recent contretemps), which I understand is unwillingly caught up in these current realities. I like talking with students about ideas. I like teaching. And by the way, it wasn't *my* students who marched against me and filed complaints. It was other students, whom I'd never met. My own students I adore—chastely, of course, and from afar.

Still, as you've probably gathered, going through a Title IX investigation—though my case was nothing compared to what others have been through (I still have a job, at least for the moment)—has made me a little mad and possibly a little dangerous: transformed from a harmless ironist into an aspiring whistleblower. High-flown terms like *due process* now spout from my cynic's lips, as though principles really mattered and something should be done to save higher ed from its saviors. It's just these sorts of unintended consequences that a more *psychologically shrewd* band of zealots could have predicted. I mean, having been hauled up on complaints once, what do I have to lose? "Confidentiality"? "Conduct befitting a professor"? Kiss my ass.

In other words, thank you to my accusers: unwitting collaborators, accidental muses.

1

The Accusation Factory

FANTASIES AND REALITIES

Wading into the Mess

For students, campuses have always been venues for coming of age, which typically includes adopting rash ideas, living on an emotional teeter-totter, sexual experimentation, erotic confusion, and acting out on adults in self-righteous ways.

For professors, campuses are where we work, and our jobs are increasingly on the line: an offended student complains about what you thought was a harmless joke and wham, where's the next mortgage payment coming from? Harmless joke? Forget it. The professoriate has been transformed into a sexually suspicious class—would-be harassers all, sexual predators in waiting. Why else the rash of new regulations devised to keep us in line? Avoid "unnecessary references to parts of the body" warns a recent directive from the commissars of sex on my campus. Also: sexual graffiti, sexual humor, and obscene gestures, not to mention sexual assault. Thanks for the advice.

As everyone knows, there's an unprecedented level of sexuality on public display in the culture (viz: the Internet), and an unprecedented level of offended sensibilities on campuses. Campus culture is at once bawdier than ever, at least for the students (random drunken hookups on weekends), and more censorious than ever for all of us (speech codes and hypersensitivity during the week). The reigning versions of student feminism are a mess, a hodgepodge of gender progress and gendered conventionality: demands for female sexual equity on the one hand (fucking and drinking like the guys); extremes of sexual suspicion and injury on the other. Emotional vulnerability runs high and introspection runs low, making campus life messy for student and professor alike, though mostly for different reasons.

Sex on campus isn't just confusing, it's schizophrenic. Into this mess steps officialdom. It would be tough to say what's messier, the sexual situation on campus or the insane measures being foisted on us to straighten everything out.

Here's a capsule summary. In 2011 the Department of Education's Office for Civil Rights (OCR) expanded Title IX's mandate from gender discrimination to encompass sexual misconduct (everything from sexual harassment, to coercion, to assault, to rape), issuing guidelines so vague that I could be accused of "creating a hostile environment on campus" for writing an essay. These vague guidelines (never subjected to any congressional review) take the form of what are called, with faux cordiality, "Dear Colleague" letters—note the nebulously threatening inflections of overempowered civil servants everywhere.

The Dear Colleague era has been disastrous for anyone who cares about either education or democracy, beginning with the manner in which these guidelines were implemented: with a tire iron. Colleges and universities are bludgeoned into compliance because "Ed" threatens to withdraw federal funding from institutions found deficient, thus encouraging extremes of compliance. In 2013, my own school received roughly $350 million in federal funding, 70 percent of its research funds for the year, I learned online.

The legal challenges to Title IX are mounting: there are cases accusing schools of trampling on due process, there are cases alleging gender bias against men, there are cases arguing that the low standard of proof demanded by the Department of Education in Title IX cases ("preponderance of evidence") is inherently unfair to the accused. The preponderance issue may sound obscure, but if you're one of the *25 million or so people* working or studying on an American campus—a not insignificant chunk of the populace—it's the standard of proof that will apply if or when you're accused of something. In other words, a 50.01 percent certainty of guilt. ("Fifty-fifty plus a feather" is how our university's Title IX officer put it.) Note that being accused doesn't mean you've actually done anything, but given the low bar for a guilty finding and the utter capriciousness of the process, an accusation itself pretty much suffices to constitute preponderance, as we'll see.

So long to niceties such as presumption of innocence. Hello to campus as penal colony.

If you get the idea that the process is stacked against the accused, law professors around the country agree with you, and have been circulating open letters protesting the rampant rights-violations and kangaroo court procedures. The specifics vary from school to school (and are often different for students and faculty), but typically the accusee doesn't know the precise charges, doesn't know what the evidence is, and can't confront witnesses. Many campuses don't even allow the accusee to present a defense, such as introducing text messages from a complainant that contradict his or her statements.

The Department of Education responds that the Dear Colleague letters are merely "guidance" and don't carry the force of law, though this is beyond disingenuous, since schools seen as insufficiently vigilant face being put on the "OCR watchlist" and subjected to federal investigation. Schools that are too *fair* toward the accused—for instance, using the "clear and convincing" standard of proof rather than the lower bar of "preponderance" demanded by Dear Colleague—will soon find OCR investigators descending on their campuses.

The cost of an OCR investigation is enormous. It can last two to four years, and those in the know say the process typically costs a school $200,000 to $350,000. Stanford, Princeton, Cornell, and Harvard have all faced at least three investigations each. As of this writing, there have been 321 investigations since 2011, with 270 currently ongoing at over 190 different schools, and the numbers are climbing. A low-end calculation of the overall cost to higher education exceeds $60 million—and that's the price tag for investigations alone, leaving aside the hundreds of millions spent yearly on *attempted* compliance.

One question is whether OCR's actions are themselves legal; critics (mostly Republicans) say the Dear Colleague letters enacted sweeping regulatory changes without first going through the notice-and-comment procedures required by the Administrative Procedure Act, which was enacted in 1946 and designed to prevent governmental agencies from foisting laws cooked up in secret on an unsuspecting public. But colleges and universities facing OCR investigations are too afraid to push back—no college presidents have dared stand up to OCR, and they're the only ones who can.* (The reason is that they're predominantly men and can't risk it, one college president I spoke to said, not for attribution.) The safer path is to simply throw everyone accused of anything under the bus. Except then your school gets sued, generally by aggrieved male students found guilty of things they say they didn't do; over a hundred and fifty such suits are currently wending their way through the courts. (Hundreds of others have been settled—one educational insurance company alone paid $36 million in settlements to falsely accused male students between 2006 and 2010.) A New York attorney known for handling such cases, including one pending against the Department of Education itself, says he averages an inquiry a day from male students who've been railroaded by the process. But it takes deep pockets for a student to sue: a minimum of a hundred thousand dollars, and up to a million to bring a case before a jury, one attorney told me.

Of course there are also a handful of lawsuits against schools accused of doing too little when it comes to Title IX enforcement, and in some cases they *have* done disgracefully little. UCLA recently settled a lawsuit (for $460,000) brought by two graduate students whose complaints about being sexually harassed by the same history professor—forcible kissing, groping, and repeated sexual advances—the school had inexplicably ignored. In other cases, the accuser is unhappy with the outcome of an adjudi-

---

* Actually one just has, on religious freedom grounds. Oklahoma Wesleyan University recently joined a federal lawsuit challenging the 2011 Dear Colleague letter, because OCR is enforcing teachings that are "the antithesis of Christian beliefs concerning sexual behavior."

cation. Harvard is currently being sued by a female student who said her ex-boyfriend abused her and Harvard hadn't done enough, despite interviewing her six times, the accusee three times, speaking to seventeen other witnesses, and reviewing text and email messages. The woman charges Harvard with showing "deliberate indifference" to her case.

So nothing here is clear cut, including the 2011 Dear Colleague letter itself, which cites, as justification for the sweeping new measures, "deeply troubling statistics" indicating that "about 1 in 5 women are victims of completed or attempted sexual assault while in college." The stat has been widely contested, including by the authors of the study from which the numbers derive. I'm not someone fascinated by statistics, but I had the good luck to hear a riveting (it's true) presentation by Callie Rennison, formerly a senior statistician at the Bureau of Justice Statistics, now a professor at the University of Colorado Denver, comparing the methodologies of major surveys on campus assault that all, it turns out, vary greatly in terms of questions asked, response rates, whether the results were nationally representative, and time frame. Some of her presentation was a little technical—did the survey account for "telescoping," which can increase sexual violence estimates from 10 to 50 percent?—but her overall point was that the enormous variation in estimates across participating universities means that any attempt to come up with a national rate of sexual violence (one in five, or one in four) is simplistic and misleading. There's not even standardized language among researchers when it comes to what "rape," "sexual assault," or even "college student" means.

Rennison was also a bit tough on the 2007 Campus Sexual Assault Study, the one cited in the Dear Colleague letter. Though it has some good points, the findings aren't nationally representative, and the one-in-five number rolls together completed rapes and other forms of assault such as forced kissing or unwanted groping. That stat also doesn't distinguish between on- and off-campus assaults—in fact, college students are more likely to be assaulted off campus than on. (They also suffer sexual violence at rates lower than their non-college counterparts, as has been widely pointed out.)

I'd already read various dissents about the one-in-five estimates: in contrast to the 20 percent figure, Emily Yoffe, writing in *Slate* in December 2014, reviewed all the research and came up with a 0.27 percent sexual assault rate for 2012, based on both reported and unreported assaults. But during Rennison's talk, something else was nagging at me. After the conference, I emailed her to ask, apologizing if it was a dumb question: "Is there evidence that sexual assault on campus has gone *up?*" The impression we're left with from the relentless rape culture drumbeat is that sexual assault has reached a new all-time high on campus, but reading through the surveys, I couldn't see any evidence of that.

Rennison kindly emailed back that the question was, of course, a bit complex to answer, given the non-comparability of the available data and the poorly designed wording of questions about rape prior to 1992. (The National Crime Victimization Survey didn't even ask if rape victims, or any victims, were college students until 1995.) Her best answer, using other types of crime as a guide, was that since roughly 1992–93 other violent crime rates have plummeted, and there was "zero reason to suspect that rape or sexual assault on campus would be different than what we see with other types of violence." There was also no evidence that rates of non-reporting have gone up over time. Someone might argue that violence that happens primarily to women follows a different pattern, she added, but intimate partner violence (also committed primarily against women) has followed the same pattern of decline since the early 1990s. She said she'd be surprised if any statisticians disagreed with this overall picture.

The question becomes whether, as with off-campus crime, sexual assault as traditionally defined may have actually gone *down*, while what *counts* as sexual assault keeps expanding. There doesn't seem to be any way of answering this question statistically, though in the chapters that follow we'll see that what counts as sexual assault is indeed being exponentially expanded, usually behind closed doors.

Raising questions about the definition of sexual assault is, however, verboten—and when I say verboten, I mean that doing so can mean losing your job, as happened to a professor named David Barnett, whose story I'll be getting to. His case is a cautionary tale for me, needless to say. As someone who gets a paycheck from an institution of higher learning (not a particularly high one, but still), acclimating to these new realities sometimes feels like being a twenty-first-century Gulliver, that is, if Gulliver had awoken to find himself shipwrecked on an atoll of sanctimony where bureaucracy had supplanted education, and slogans have replaced thinking.

I hear the term *sex-positive* a lot from my students. What I find myself wanting to say is that the older you get, the more you realize that sex is always going to be messy, and sometimes even negative (which is what's both appealing and also distressing about it)—and messy in ways that embarrass everyone's good intentions, like a delinquent friend who spits in your face after you post his bail money. The messiness resides as much in your own desires as in the gross ones other people foist on you. There's no honest sex-positivity; it's all just a lot less simple than that.

Freud makes the point in the "Dora" case, which centers on an unwelcome sexual advance (an unwanted kiss the teenage Dora can't seem to get past), that it's usually not external events we can't get over. It's the internal ones we're in denial about that form the basis of our accusations. "A string of reproaches against other people leads one to suspect a string of self-reproaches with the same content." It's the question I'd like to put to the two campus accusers featured in the chapters to follow: Is there something (or someone) you're leaving out of the story?

A Selective Approach to Facts

A crush on a professor used to be the most ordinary thing in the world. Now, at least in public discourse, Eros runs strictly in the opposite direction: predatory professors foisting themselves on innocent and unwilling students, who lack any desires of their own. The question is what becomes of young women learning to negotiate their sexual attractions and conflicts in a campus culture that promotes so much dissimulating about them?

In the fall of 2011, a Northwestern freshman I'll call Eunice Cho, a journalism major, enrolled in a class titled Philosophy of Cyberspace, taught by Peter Ludlow. A few months after the class ended, in early February 2012, Cho emailed Ludlow: "Hi Professor Ludlow. I just wanted to let you know that I am going to Fluxfest in Chicago on Friday . . . I heard it's going to be amazing. You should totally come, too." Flux Fest is an annual avant-garde performance art event tangentially related to *Second Life*, the online virtual community that had been the theme of the course.

It wasn't unusual for Cho to contact Ludlow: she'd emailed him frequently while enrolled in his class, sometimes about assignments, but about other things, too. She'd emailed after the first class to tell him she enjoyed his lecture and that she'd loved playing virtual reality games since elementary school. She emailed a few weeks later to say she was in "an extreme state of panic" because she'd missed a discussion section (led by a teaching assistant). She emailed over Thanksgiving break about a virtual Thanksgiving dinner of pixilated sweet potato casserole she'd "eaten" on *Second Life*. In one email, she told him she'd Googled his name and learned how famous he was, having come across an article on MTV's website voting him one of the ten most influential video gamers in cyberspace, adding that she couldn't "help but get more and more creeped out" by his "extremely influential cyber power." Cho would later state that she'd kept her interactions and communications with Ludlow "professional."

Though well known as a philosopher of language, Ludlow had been gravitating toward more cutting-edge research areas related to cyberculture: "hacktivism" (that is, online activism like WikiLeaks), cyber rights, and ethics in virtual communities, academic areas certainly new to philosophy. He'd been especially influential as an early theorist on *Second Life*. A 3-D virtual world started in 2003, at its peak it boasted a million users, known as Residents, who create avatars and build vast virtual cities, unencumbered by the constraints of physical reality—teleporting is possible, also virtual sex. *Second Life* has its own currency, called Linden dollars, named for the software's developer, Linden Lab; more entrepreneurial Residents have figured out how to make actual money, starting businesses and speculating in *Second Life* real estate.

Beyond the financial possibilities, the appeal of *Second Life* is its open-endedness: Residents can invent new worlds instead of inheriting one handed down by developer overlords. They can create complex governance structures and new ways of relating and socializing with others in the community, though old ways of relating (aggression, misogyny) haven't exactly been relegated to the dustbins of the "meat world," as cyber habitués refer to "real life." Ludlow conducted class in *Second Life*, meaning students did assignments and held class meetings in a 3-D digital landscape, building avatars who examined philosophical and political topics.

The class had run from September through December, and word leaked out to the meat world that intriguing things were happening. A student journalist attempted to capture the tenor in an online article, describing Ludlow as "an enigma with a dual persona," one who split his time between the "mainland" and the online virtual world, where his avatar was named Urizenus Sklar. In the mainland classroom, he observed, Ludlow wore Gucci loafers and had a Penrose triangle tattooed on his left forearm—not your typical philosophy professor perhaps, though he was also described as treading the line "between trendy and sloppy," which sounds closer to type. Ludlow was the kind of teacher who gets called "charismatic" on student evaluations: hip (despite being in his mid-fifties), political, unpretentiously enthusiastic about his subject, and eloquent about the subversive possibilities of new technologies. He calls everyone "dude," regardless of gender.

Though he still wrote traditional philosophical articles, his cyberculture work made him a sought-after speaker—indeed Ludlow had been recruited to rejuvenate the department, according to the chair (who would eventually become a foe). At the time of the scandal, he'd recently been awarded an endowed chair, the most prestigious professorial rank, though his new title, the John Evans Professor in Moral and Intellectual Philosophy, would later come to seem like unintended irony. (He'd be stripped of it eventually, in any case.)

He'd also earned notoriety in the gaming community for starting an online newspaper called the *Alphaville Herald*, which covered news in a previous virtual reality game he was involved in, *The Sims*. (*The Sims* bills itself as a "life simulation video game series," whereas the creators of *Second Life* reject the word *game* and see their creation in loftier, social-experiment terms.) But things turned sour when Ludlow wrote a muckraking article criticizing exploitative role playing (violence, underage prostitution) in *The Sims* community and accusing the game's owner, Electronic Arts, the behemoth video game developer—revenues now exceed $4 billion—of not doing enough to root out corruption and crime. Electronic Arts didn't take this well and responded by shuttering Ludlow's account. So much for freedom of the press in cyberspace.

Cho's emails to Ludlow continued throughout the quarter she was his student: She wrote requesting sources for a journalism assignment she was writing about *Second Life*, addressing him as "Professor Uri." She met him during office hours a few times. ("I want to ask you something I'll drop by Wednesday," she'd email casually.) She interviewed him for another journalism assignment, and Ludlow helped her get it published in the *Alphaville Herald*. Once, she emailed asking him how to get twenty Linden dollars, adding that she was "real life broke and second life broke," though Ludlow didn't require students to acquire Lindens for the class, and the Linden-to-dollar exchange rate was around ten cents.

After the class ended, and throughout January, Cho continued emailing Ludlow to update him on her work interviewing artists working in *Second Life*. When she wrote him in February about the Flux Fest event, Ludlow responded, mentioning two other art events the same evening he planned on going to. He offered to drive them both from campus—the events were a half-hour drive away, in downtown Chicago.

Cho wrote back, "Sounds amazing. I'd love to," and "What

time should we go and where can we meet?" It would later become a matter of debate whether "You should totally come, too" was an invitation, or if Cho's email had been strictly informational— she was adamant that Ludlow had invited her, not the other way around.

They met at his office that February afternoon, as previously arranged, and walked to his car. The plan was to hit the Flux Fest exhibit and then the other gallery openings he'd mentioned. Cho was working on a video documentary for one of her journalism classes, and Ludlow had said he'd introduce her to curators and performers she could interview. When asked at her deposition why she'd accepted his invitation, Cho replied that campus culture encourages professors and students to engage in out-of-classroom academic activities.

Maybe so, but attraction is also a funny business. Cho would later indicate that she found Ludlow old and disgusting—yet there she was on her way to his car. Disgust itself isn't an uncomplicated emotion, something I often discuss with my students, since what kind of writer can you be without a working theory of disgust? Managing the interplay of attraction and repulsion is one of the larger problems we social beings are faced with, every human's little quagmire to navigate. When Cho wrote to Ludlow that she couldn't help getting "creeped out" by his "extremely influential cyber power," I suspect she was expressing something similar: the byplay of desire and repugnance, excitement and disavowal. Such contradictory emotions aren't all that unusual in the annals of teacher-student relations, though, for whatever reason (reasons I suspect she herself wasn't especially attuned to), Cho felt this quagmire of hers was something she needed to express to Ludlow himself.

I believe this is known, in the wider culture, as "flirtation." Confessing one's feelings for or about someone *to* that person, especially when you haven't previously been in a "discussing feelings" kind of mode, is a way of opening that conversation. It creates intimacy. Our campus's Title IX officer, Joan Slavin, would decree that Cho's emails did *not* "indicate a crush or romantic interest on her part," after Ludlow raised the possibility. Cho simply wanted to make "a good impression," Slavin ruled. Perhaps she did, but to insist that's all there was to it is to exhibit the psychological acuity of a mollusk.

I did myself wonder whether having met in a venue where fantasy and reality overlapped, a class conducted in the virtual landscape of *Second Life,* might have colored subsequent events between Ludlow and Cho. "In a setting where the point is to play out fantasies, there is little agreement among players about the real-world consequences of their online actions," a *New York Times* account of Ludlow's run-in with Electronic Arts put it. (The story had caused a stir in the non-virtual world too.) Cho echoed these sentiments in her own admiring article about Ludlow: "By founding The Alphaville Herald . . . Ludlow had created yet another indication that the boundaries between the virtual world and the real world had become more indefinite."

In that Ludlow would eventually be expelled from our little community too, I'd been intrigued to read about his previous expulsion from Alphaville, his *Sims* hometown, and the first community whose authorities he'd offended. It was an odd prequel of events to come. Claiming that Ludlow had violated the rules—he'd violated a technicality by linking to his own newspaper's site from the *The Sims* site—Electronic Arts exiled him from his virtual home and confiscated his property;

even his two virtual cats were seized. Closing Ludlow's account also erased his avatar—in the world of the game, the company essentially murdered him.

By the time I met him, a decade or so later, he'd been banned from the Northwestern campus, erased from the philosophy department website, and had had to sell his real-world downtown Chicago condominium in Marina Towers, overlooking the river—his legal bills were in the hundreds of thousands of dollars. I asked him if there was any connection between his having been expelled from two communities in one lifetime, but he deflected the question, pointing out that technically he'd resigned this time around. Since he was on the verge of being terminated (or so he and everyone else assumed), it struck me as a distinction without a difference.

Though neither Ludlow nor Cho regarded their planned outing as a date (at least neither ever acknowledged regarding it as a date), as of February 10, 2012, when the excursion took place, there was no regulation at our university prohibiting professors and students from dating; the Great Prohibition happened two years later. In 2012 it was still assumed that students over the age of consent could make their own romantic decisions, which shows just how fast things can change.

On the drive downtown, Ludlow and Cho talked about normal stuff, then hit the first art event, the one Cho had suggested—but it turned out not to have *Second Life* content. Ludlow asked if Cho was hungry. They went to a restaurant called GT Fish & Oyster, and from there to a succession of other art events and a bar, and later, around midnight, to a jazz club called Andy's.

They ended up at Ludlow's apartment and slept in the same bed, clothed. Both agree they didn't have sex.

They disagree on everything else. Ludlow says that he wanted to send Cho home in a taxi after the last gallery opening—it was snowing, and he didn't want to drive—but Cho asked if she could crash on his couch. He said she could stay in his guest room—he later acknowledged that this was incredibly poor judgment on his part.

Cho says Ludlow dissuaded her from going back to Evanston even though there was a party on campus at 9:30 she'd been invited to. Ludlow told her Northwestern was lame and she shouldn't go to the stupid party, they could "go hard" together. Ludlow says he never said any of this. According to Cho, by the end of the evening, she'd drunk so much she was lapsing in and out of consciousness and incapable of making any decisions; and she didn't know how she ended up at Ludlow's apartment.

She says she woke up to find him groping her. He says that never happened. She says he'd touched her back and tried to kiss her earlier, in the bar. He says she propositioned him, and he'd told her to "chill."

When I look back on things now, trying to figure out how my own involvement in this mess got under way, I believe it started with a jab of irritation. In early 2014, I read something that irritated me. This isn't so unusual in itself—I'm more or less perpetually irritated—the notable thing is remembering this instance so clearly. The upside of irritation is that it can be a sort of creative goad at times, at least to the extent that what prevents you from turning your attention away becomes your default subject matter (or monomania, which is what makes irritated people themselves so irritating).

The critic Roland Barthes has a theory of what he calls the "punctum," a small detail in a photograph that grabs you in an intense way that you don't necessarily understand. It's like a puncture in the surface, an imaginary opening that your psyche tumbles into—or that's how I read him. (Barthes can be a bit elliptical.) For me, this punctum didn't arrive in a photograph. It was a detail in a news story about events on my campus. Why did this detail jab me? Because something about it seemed implausible? Maybe a deeper reason was that it suddenly tumbled me back to my youth, and the freedoms and adventures that shaped me into becoming who I am—there's a Barthesean theme: the melancholy of being who you are—that is, a writer so dangerously out of step with current campus verities that she'd soon be caught up in a series of contentious events that anyone else would have run a mile from.

The jabbing detail whirred by fast: a female student was charging that a male professor had forced her to drink, which led to her trying to kill herself. There were other details, and further charges about which I'd later learn, but the additional charges all rested on this initial charge—and the story just didn't add up. The news reports took for granted that it did, but going along with that required placing my intelligence on hold. Another way of putting it was that I was being asked to believe a lie, though maybe *lie* is too strong a word. Maybe it would be kinder to say I was being asked to sign on to a fantasy presented as reality. You can see how this detail rankled me—I can't even find the right language to express how emblematic it seemed of the wrongheaded direction of things on our campus and around the country, which I'd mostly tried to ignore, but this demand to *stop thinking entirely* (and the implication that any right-thinking citizen would), was too much to go along with.

The rankled feeling was still festering a year or so later when the *Chronicle* invited me to expound upon campus sexual politics, and as the essay unfolded in my mind, I found myself returning to this scenario. I didn't know the professor who'd been accused of forcing the student to drink, but I do know the world of professors and students pretty well. I also know the limits of professorial power, and I simply didn't believe in a reality in which a professor can force a student to drink. How would you enforce this: report the student to the not-drinking committee?

Let's say for the sake of argument that certain professors possess outsize charisma—having once been a young female student myself, I'm familiar with such lures (and the attendant attraction-repulsion they can engender), but even lots of charisma can't force a person to drink. I suppose a professor could *pressure* a student to drink. Still, there's the sinister implication that *if* a professor could, he'd *want* to. Why exactly? Oh right—so that he could force her into sex.

Not only was this forced-drinking tale rather tinny, it was a definite uptick in the already heightened tenor of sexual paranoia and accusatory mania on campus: if this kind of allegation could stick, anything would stick. It was also complete melodrama, this world of dastardly men with the nefarious power to bend passive damsels to their wills, a world out of storybooks. I understand that at the moment—post Bill Cosby, after #MeToo—every male on the planet is presumed to have knock-out drops and sinister intentions up his sleeve. But it's also still the case that people are sometimes accused of things they haven't done.

Joan Slavin, the Title IX officer, first learned about Cho's evening with Ludlow after being alerted by one of Cho's journalism instructors that Cho was in the hospital, sent by the student health service after telling them she'd tried to kill herself by jumping into Lake Michigan.

Cho had called two of her instructors following the suicide attempt and managed to reach one who, afterward, emailed Slavin in a panic: "Joan, please give me a call as soon as you can. . . . This sounds like a case of a faculty member abusing his position of authority to take advantage of a freshman." She conferred with Cho's other instructor to determine which of them should call the police.

It's not clear what crime they thought had been committed. Cho had assured the instructor she hadn't been raped. There had been an "inappropriate relationship" with a well-known and powerful male faculty member, she said. According to the instructor's notes on the conversation, Cho said she'd been to five bars with a male professor two nights before, he'd spent about six hundred dollars on alcohol, and he'd forced her to drink. Because she was so drunk and didn't know what else to do, she'd gone with him to his apartment. There had been kissing, but nothing else. The instructor told Cho she was brave for coming forward.

Although Cho wouldn't reveal the professor's name, as everyone knows, the best way of creating intrigue is to withhold crucial details, and it didn't take long for the instructor—she didn't teach journalism for nothing—to figure out Ludlow's identity. In fact, all she had to do was go to Cho's Facebook page, which led her to Ludlow's Facebook page, where the details of the evening (Cho videotaping and interviewing artists at the various art events) were posted for the world to see in an album labeled "art nite."

This being the age of social media, both Cho and Ludlow spent much of the evening documenting what they did, ate, and drank, and posting photos online. It's clear Ludlow thought the photos were innocent, or why post them? Though they displayed nothing untoward, they caused intense alarm for Cho's instructors. Merely taking photos of Cho (herself conducting interviews) was seen as sexually creepy.

You get the impression that Cho's histrionic state was contagious—everyone who came in contact with her got caught up in it, as would the entire campus eventually. The details of the "inappropriate relationship" with the "powerful professor" would also heighten the more Cho retold the story over the next few months and years, mirroring the mounting campus hysteria nationwide. Pressure to drink became anger and threats—maybe Ludlow had even drugged her, Cho would later suggest. What stayed constant was the melodramatic framing of the narrative. From the moment Cho dialed her instructor, the endangered damsel–powerful predator story snapped into place, and those preassigned roles would dictate what questions could be asked and how the story was understood.

Of course the suicide attempt only amplified these themes. If Cho had tried to kill herself, clearly Ludlow was a monster. This sequence of causes and effects was itself cast in stone, including in Slavin's eventual Title IX report:

> *Complainant has been under extreme emotional stress due to the events of the evening of February 10. She testified that she attempted to drown herself and was admitted as an inpatient in the psychiatric ward for several days following the evening with Respondent. She has been undergoing treatment and counseling with psychologists subsequent to the event and reports that she is now suffering from posttraumatic stress disorder. Her academic and personal life has suffered as a result of her evening with Respondent.*

In the official version of events, causality can run in only one direction: Ludlow alone can be the prime mover; Cho can only be someone things happen *to*. Further questions are automatically foreclosed—for instance, was it possible that Cho was emotionally distressed or unstable *prior* to the evening with Ludlow, which might have affected how she reacted to, or recounted, what did or didn't transpire between them? Don't ask. To the contrary, Cho's account of the evening would be seen as all the *more* credible in light of the suicide attempt, since it cemented the familiar story about dastardly men and helpless damsels even more securely in place.

Note that this is a story that can also prove financially advantageous under the right circumstances. On her first meeting with Slavin, Cho said that her mother had told her they should "lawyer up," and asked Slavin whether filing charges on campus precluded her from filing a civil suit. Indeed, Cho soon hired a lawyer, who sent a demand letter to Ludlow requesting an unspecified amount of compensation for damages. Ludlow ignored the letter. Cho then hired a personal injury lawyer on contingency, who filed suit against Ludlow under the Illinois Gender Violence Act, seeking punitive damages and further damages for emotional distress. She also filed a federal suit against the university, demanding that her tuition be reimbursed, along with compensation for emotional distress and future medical bills. Ludlow responded by filing a defamation suit against Cho.

The downside of bringing these suits for Cho was that more probing questions were going to be put to her than were asked during the campus investigation. As we'll see, the sorts of narratives that are routinely ratified on campus don't necessarily hold up under more stringent scrutiny.

To begin with, that suicide attempt. The first time anyone raised questions about it was at Cho's deposition in her civil suit against Ludlow, when his lawyer, Kristen Case, pressed Cho on the fine points of jumping into the lake in mid-February. To many of these queries, Cho replies with a curt "I don't remember." She doesn't remember what she was wearing, she doesn't remember whether there was ice on the lake when she jumped in. She does remember that it was freezing. Case presses: "You don't remember hitting ice when you jumped in?" Watching the video of the deposition, I noticed that Cho doesn't even pause to try to remember (or to appear to be trying to remember); the response comes instantly. Eventually she elaborates: she wasn't in the water long because when she jumped in, a guy on the beach saw her.

"He was just like, what are you doing there? I'm going to call the cops. Like, what are you doing there, it's like freezing. And

I was super embarrassed, and I got out of there immediately because I didn't want him to call the cops."

Q: Okay. How did you get out of the water?
A: I started swimming toward the shore. It wasn't even that long of a swim.
Q: And then once you got out of the water, what did you do?
A: I darted home. I didn't even stop to have a conversation with that guy because I was way too embarrassed.

Cho's dorm was a five-minute walk from the lake, but she didn't go back into her room. She stayed outside, not wanting the security guard to see her drenched hair and clothing and start asking questions. Case asks how long Cho hung around outside.

A: I don't know. Maybe like an hour. I really don't know.
Q: But you recall you were dry by the time you went back inside?

She wasn't fully dry, Cho said, but she decided not to go change. Instead, she went to the bathroom behind the security desk and called two of her professors.

Q: Okay. Did you have frostbite or anything?
A: No.
Q: Okay. Any hypothermia?
A: No, I didn't have to get medical attention for it at all.
Q: You said you called your professors when you got back to your dorm, from the bathroom?
A: Yes.

Q: Did you call them from a pay phone or a cell phone?

A: Cell phone.

Q: Okay. Where was your cell phone when you were jumping into the lake?

At this point comes a long pause while Cho gropes for an explanation. On the video, you see her flummoxed by Case's questions and floundering for answers. She hadn't had the phone on her, she eventually explains. Case asks where it was.

A: I remember, like—so wait. Sorry. If I can—sorry, I'm trying to like, remember everything.

Q: Okay.

A: So what happened was that—ok, sorry. What happened was that I had a bag with me. I didn't wear the bag when I jumped in.

Q: So where did you leave [the bag]?

A: It was on the pier.

Q: You left it on the pier?

A: Yeah. And I also had a jacket too. That I left on the pier because I was cold. Honestly, like—it's like, you know, I didn't like jump in with my bag and my coat on.

Q: You took your coat off?

A: Yes. So the cell phone wasn't damaged at all because it was never in the water.

Q: Ok. So after you swam from the pier to the beach—

A: Yeah, I took my stuff and I left.

Q:—then you ran back to the pier to get your stuff?

A: Yeah. It's only a walk. I was like near it the entire time.

Q: Did the man who saw you follow you back to the pier?

A: No I don't—like to be honest, like, I don't remember where he was that he saw me but all I know is, like, it's not like he was standing there looking me right in the eye like watching me. Like, I don't—it was almost like he was like a voice. It was dark. I can't—he wasn't there. It wasn't like he was following me. I think he was just seeing everything from afar.

This man on the pier sounds ghostly, dreamlike. Perhaps someone who's tried to kill herself will be necessarily blurry on the details, but when does blurriness cross the line into invention? For anyone cursed enough to have been in proximity to Lake Michigan in February—and I sure have; our campus abuts the lake—Cho's story of jumping in the water and then walking around outside for an hour is tough to buy.

I examined Cho's videotaped deposition testimony for clues to her character. She was twenty-one by then, and seems poised enough in a lemon Chanel-ish jacket (or Chanel via J.Crew), with large buttons and black piping, the kind of thing Audrey Hepburn might have worn with a pillbox hat if she'd been deposed in 1961. Cho speaks in flat California-nasal intonations, in tones alternating between dismissive and petulant. The flatness makes her emotions hard to read.

As it happens, there was an online "swim report" for that very same February day posted by "Steve," a local nut job—excuse me, outdoorsman—who makes it a point to swim with two friends in Lake Michigan throughout the winter (in wet suits, of course), which reads in part:

We were already suited up, so we donned our hoods and gloves and quickly trotted out to the ladder and got into the drink. . . .

I slogged through the floes {of ice} as fast as I could . . . we all realized that ice had formed on us during the swim and had accumulated on our hoods, gloves, and booties. In short, the lake was slowly and insidiously encasing us in ice. . . . We were all quite frozen after the swim, and I had a particularly nasty afterdrop {in body temperature}. I bundled up in multiple layers of clothing but still shivered pretty vigorously for about 15 minutes.

It makes Cho not remembering whether there was ice on the lake also hard to buy. Everything in this case hinged on her credibility: it was her word against Ludlow's about what happened that evening. The Title IX report consistently finds Cho the more truthful of the two. If the details of the suicide attempt become this rickety under questioning, what other details of her story may have been less than solid?

The swim report wasn't part of Ludlow's defense in the campus charges, by the way, because during Slavin's investigation he was never told what the evidence against him was. He didn't know, for instance, that Cho had accused him of groping her in the elevator ride up to his apartment; if he'd known, he'd have been able to procure the security tapes from his building, which, he said, would have proved that nothing like that happened. By the time he learned about the elevator claim, it was months later (upon reading Slavin's report), and the tapes had long since been erased.

The journalism instructor Cho phoned after she emerged from the lake (in her version of events) made an interesting observation in her notes. Of Cho and the unnamed professor, she wrote, "She seemed to put a lot of stock in his (real or imagined) fame and power, which I got the sense he promoted."

Ludlow's "real or imagined power" had definitely been an object of Cho's fascination for months, as she herself had confessed to Ludlow: recall, she was "creeped out" by his cyberpower. If Cho was girlishly overinvested in Ludlow's stature, the older women she consulted seemed similarly disposed: fixated on and repelled by a fantasy of powerful, brutish men. It's one of the tragicomic elements of the campus situation that the guys onto whom such fantasies are projected are often as hapless as they come.

Did Ludlow "promote" his real or imagined power? To answer the question adequately would require a far more nuanced assessment of what power *is* and how it works on campus than anyone seemed prepared to embark on. Instead, power is utterly mystified. I say this, in part, because if a student thinks a professor has such unlimited powers that he can compel her to drink or retaliate if she doesn't, then our students have been very badly educated about the nature *and limits* of institutional power.

Everywhere on campuses today you find scholars whose work elaborates sophisticated models of power and agency. It would be hard to overstate the influence, across disciplines, of the French philosopher and social theorist Michel Foucault, whose signature idea was that power has no permanent address or valence; its exercises are diffuse and dispersed. The campus situation itself is a prime example.

Here's a random glimpse. Not long ago I overheard a conversation between a student and a young untenured male professor down the hall. (His door was open, of course—it had better be, especially if you're male.) The student, voice raised, was arguing over an A-minus final grade. I'd had this student myself; she'd excoriated me by email and on the course evaluations for mistakes she said I'd made in the design of the class. She was someone who thought of herself as disempowered—in fact she was consumed with the idea—yet acted like a bulldozer. If I'd been untenured, I'd have been worried about engaging in the confrontation that was going on down the hall: the reality is that it's far more likely for a student to derail a professor's career these days than the other way around. In fact, students can be quite ruthless in trying to bring down the objects of their enmity, including fighting (with increasing success) to fire professors whose views, demeanor, or humor they find not to their liking.

Yet, for the bureaucrats writing our campus codes, only the crudest versions of top-down power are imaginable. Students are putty in the hands of an all-powerful professoriate. According to Cho's complaints against Ludlow, this was indeed how she saw herself: virtually a rag doll. If so, my question is the extent to which this sense of vulnerability is *learned* on campus. The new campus codes don't just enforce disabling myths and fantasies about power, they also produce a new host of pathologies around power. A student trying to get a professor fired over a joke or some other passing offense is someone who utterly and callously misunderstands the consequences of leaving someone else (often with dependents to support) jobless; and someone who has, in fact, seized power while hiding behind the fiction of powerlessness.*

---

* I'm thinking of cases like that of Teresa Buchanan, a tenured associate professor of education at Louisiana State University who was fired in 2015, after twenty years of teaching, for swearing in class and making a joke about sex

My own sense, when Ludlow and I eventually met, wasn't that he played up his power so much as that he imagined he could play it down. He had a misplaced egalitarianism; whether that sprang from some philosophical or ethical conviction, I have no idea. I'm not saying he was without vanity, but he seemed to think he could move up and down the social pecking order at will: keynote speaker at international philosophical conferences one moment, schmoozing with undergrads the next. Of course, he was also someone accustomed to roaming a digital landscape in avatar form, where agelessness is the norm and stature is virtual—even gender can be switched at will. But in the "meat world" too, he preferred to think that professional hierarchies and other earthly constraints were nonfactors. It's not that he's naïve about sexism or gender inequities, though I suspect he thinks treating women as equals temporarily brackets the issue. In a campus culture that assumes every male professor is an abuser-of-power-in-waiting, it may be this particular irreality that ulti-mately brought him down.

Speaking of reality checks, a crucial slice of reality ig-nored in this case was that Ludlow actually *had no* institu-tional power over Cho. She wasn't his student any longer that evening in February; the course had ended. She wasn't in his department, or his college, for that matter. What possible repercussions could he have visited on her, supposing he'd wanted to, if she'd said she wouldn't be drinking? He had no say over her future. Maybe he could have refused to write her

---

declining in long-term relationships. There have been a cavalcade of similar stories in the last few years.

a letter of recommendation had she requested one, but that's pretty much it.

Needless to say, the *limits* of Ludlow's power weren't part of the story. Mystifying the unlimited power of male professors and the lengths they'll go to exercise it is a far more gripping tale. Just as Ludlow had mesmerizing powers over female students, so is the campus community ensorcelled by these latter-day captivity narratives, and fairy tales about endangered damsels.

The more we enforce these narratives on our students, the more fragile they become. Malevolently fragile? Call it a working hypothesis. Just how fragile *was* Cho? The photos from the evening in question tell a sturdy enough story: Cho holding a camera and shooting interviews, looking competent and in control. In other photos, ones that Ludlow provided Slavin, taken by someone at one of the galleries, the two of them are sitting on a couch together. Cho's laughing, looking relaxed and happy.

Cho, too, posted cell phone photos from the evening on her Instagram account, including a coffee-and–whipped cream concoction she'd later say Ludlow forced her to order. She'd say she didn't remember posting the shots until confronted with them during the deposition, and asked to explain. "I think it might have been a youthful tendency for people to document the food that they're eating because Instagram did exist back in that day." Pressed by Ludlow's lawyer, Kristen Case, to clarify what she meant, Cho says that it had been a journalistic instinct, because it was strange that her professor was buying her alcohol and she wanted to protect herself "just in case something went terribly wrong."

Case asks if she was gathering evidence, and Cho agrees that's what she was doing.

Q: If at this time you took this picture you were so worried that something bad might happen that you felt the need to document it, why didn't you walk out the door and get in a taxi?

Cho: Because I was afraid that he would retaliate against me.

When Case asks *how* Ludlow might retaliate, Cho says that since Ludlow had been published in the *New York Times*, he might warn editors that she was a horrible person and instruct them not to work with her, though she'd since realized that he didn't actually have this sort of influence in reality.

On campus, this fantasy of Ludlow-the-retaliator was taken as a given, including in Slavin's Title IX report. Due to her "perception of Respondent's prestige and position," Slavin assessed that "Cho was unable to extricate herself from the situation." Ludlow had created what a "reasonable person would perceive to be an intimidating, hostile, or offensive environment," Slavin writes, despite the fact that he hadn't actually proposed any quid pro quo arrangements, or mentioned any specifics of how he was planning to use his power to help Cho's career.

This seems contradictory. If it's Cho's *perception* of Ludlow that created the "intimidating environment," then isn't Slavin finding Ludlow responsible for Cho's fantasies about the extent of his powers? Not only is there no evidence that Ludlow's supposed powers were ever, in actuality, deployed, even Cho herself eventually acknowledged they were imaginary.

But who cares about reality? Or evidence? Asking what constitutes "evidence" in a Title IX investigation is like asking what constitutes evidence in a witch hunt. As in Salem, the accusations of post-adolescent girls still factor heavily; then as now, prosecutors based charges on "spectral shapes" seen by witnesses, which accused witches had allegedly assumed. It's precisely the way "power" functioned in Ludlow's case—spectral, an awareness, a suspicion that can't be disproved. Like the mark of the devil in Salem circa 1692, its very amorphousness is vital to its fearful effect. If the witches of Salem had the power to induce fits in children from across town, why shouldn't a modern-day witch be able to force an unwilling student to drink from across a table?

The logic of Slavin's Title IX report is similarly ethereal. Improbable assertions go unquestioned; the constraints of physical reality are irrelevant, not least Cho's wintery plunge in the lake. The accuser's credibility is assumed, the accused disbelieved at every turn.

Nor did Slavin question Cho's story that she was going in and out of consciousness throughout the evening. Off campus, the questions were more pointed. At the deposition, Ludlow's lawyer walked Cho through what she'd actually imbibed, drink by drink, establishing that she'd had at most three drinks over the course of six hours. Was that enough to cause her to lose consciousness?

Ludlow had told Slavin that Cho hadn't drunk much during the evening. Slavin ruled that Cho was more credible than Ludlow on the issue. Why? Because Cho gave detailed descriptions of exactly what both she and Ludlow drank, Slavin said, and of "the symptoms of her intoxication, including nausea, flushing, sleepiness, and confusion, and later, blacking out."

Among the details Cho provided was that Ludlow was drinking Red Bull and vodka at one of their stops. Ludlow says he'd been drinking beer. Red Bull and vodka is a notoriously disgusting student drink. If Slavin believed these details made Cho more credible, it made me wonder what social world she inhabited, because it's not one I'm familiar with.

The reason the Red Bull matters is that, at almost every turn in her investigation, Slavin found that the "preponderance of evidence" supported Cho's account, because hers was *more detailed*. I mentioned the low bar of proof mandated by the Department of Education in sexual misconduct investigations on campus. So how is "preponderance" established? In Slavin's method, preponderance rests on quantity of details, though it's not particularly clear why more details signal a true account, rather than an imaginative one.

Besides which, since Ludlow didn't know what the charges were, he wouldn't have known which details were relevant.

The details were also ratcheted up the more Cho told the story, as was the intensity of Ludlow's powerful sway over her. She'd initially told Slavin that Ludlow asked if she drank, and when she said yes, he ordered her a glass of wine. This turned into Ludlow *encouraging* her to drink. By the time she filed her lawsuits, the story was more ominous: Ludlow had *insisted* she drink, though she didn't want to; under pressure, she acquiesced.

At the deposition there was another twist: her drinks had been "unsupervised" at times. Ludlow's lawyer sounds almost bemused.

Q: So what are you thinking might have happened to that drink when it was unsupervised?
A: I am not making any accusations or saying anything for certainty, but I was feeling I was definitely going in and out of consciousness so there might have been something in my drink. I am not sure.

Q: So you think Peter Ludlow might have put something in your drink?

A: I am not making any accusations.

You can't exactly disprove an unmade accusation, yet there it is. I found myself thinking that Slavin's investigation mirrored Cho's suspicions that Ludlow drugged her drink. It's the trope of the slippery slope: if Ludlow bought Cho drinks, then he was capable of anything. I was later told that a number of feminist professors on campus suspected Ludlow had "taken a page from the Bill Cosby playbook," which is why Cho had passed out, despite, by her own account, not having drunk that much.

If Ludlow was capable of anything, Cho, by contrast, was incapable of anything. Especially when it came to sex. Among the details she imparted to Slavin was that she had a boyfriend who was a freshman and they didn't have sex, which Slavin includes in her report. The relevance is that Cho told Slavin that Ludlow had asked her if she had a boyfriend and "if she and her boyfriend 'fuck.'" Ludlow told her that she and he were ultimately going to have sex, Cho said. He disputed this, telling Slavin it had been Cho who brought up her boyfriend, asking Ludlow if he was in a relationship and if he'd date a student, and telling him she'd once dated a guy fourteen years older. Slavin concluded that Cho's account of her relationship with her boyfriend and their lack of sexual activity was more convincing than Ludlow's version.

"Who propositioned whom?" was, of course, a crucial question. Cho can come on to Ludlow, but if he came on to her, it would have been an "unwelcome advance." If Slavin reports that Cho's boyfriend was a freshman and they don't have sex, it paints a certain picture of Cho: an innocent. Things couldn't have happened the way Ludlow said *because* of Cho's innocence. Even if an innocent can still proposition a professor, the more familiar script kicked in: Ludlow was a sexual predator trying to sway Cho from the path of virtue.

This would become the official story on campus, even though off campus a more complicated picture emerged. At the deposition, Cho acknowledged that she'd had five or six older boyfriends; the current one was thirty, nine years older. She'd broken up with one boyfriend when she found out he was seeing prostitutes; also he'd tried to blackmail her. (The relevance was that Cho was seeking damages for emotional distress; Ludlow's lawyer was trying to establish that there may have been other causes for Cho's distress than her evening with Ludlow.)

At Andy's, the jazz club they visited around midnight, Cho said Ludlow started massaging her back, and the next thing she knew, he was grabbing and kissing her, putting his tongue in her mouth. Ludlow tells it differently: Cho leaned over and kissed him, and he accepted, but when she started to French kiss him he pulled away and told her to chill. He says he never massaged her back. Slavin found that the back rubbing and French kissing "most likely" happened the way Cho said, that it was initiated by Ludlow, and that Cho had been too drunk to meaningfully consent to any physical touching.

"I find it inherently implausible that Respondent told Complainant to chill and to stop kissing him," states Slavin.

Is it "inherently implausible" that Ludlow would tell Cho to stop kissing him because . . . that's not what a man would do? Because a middle-aged man is more likely to come on to a young woman than the other way around? Is this based on men Slavin knows, or just generalities about men? She seems to have firmly ingrained ideas about the ways men and women act; when Cho confirms those ideas, Slavin confirms Cho's account. For instance, according to Slavin, Ludlow told Cho that he thought she was attractive, "discussed his desire to have a romantic and sexual relationship" with her, and shared sexual information, all of which was unwelcome to her.

I'm dying to know how Slavin came to the conclusion that Ludlow wanted to have a romantic relationship with Cho. Because an evening spent drinking and going to galleries indicates a man's desire for a relationship? If so, single women of America, your problems are over.

Among the other details Cho related were Ludlow telling Cho that she should feel lucky to be at Andy's with him because "there's so many bitches that would be, like, killing to be in your spot." If Slavin buys this, maybe she thinks Ludlow doubles as a rapper in his spare time? It's not exactly the argot of the mid-fifties philosophy professor, at least not in my experience.

Once back at Ludlow's apartment, both Cho and Ludlow agree that they slept on top of the bed with their clothes on and a comforter pulled over them.

In Cho's version (or the first one), she blacked out and came to in bed to find Ludlow kissing and fondling her on top of her clothes, touching her breasts and buttocks. He told her he wanted to have sex; she says she told him she didn't want to. He told her they didn't have to have sex but eventually they would.

Ludlow adamantly denied any touching or kissing. Cho didn't pass out; they'd gone to his bedroom to watch TV, but they both fell asleep. Each slept on their own side of the bed. He says there was a pillow between them.

Cho disputes that there was a pillow. She says she woke up at 4:00 a.m. to find Ludlow's arm around her, and him spooning her. (Ludlow denies any spooning.) She went outside onto his terrace to smoke a cigarette—he'd told her not to smoke in the apartment—then she passed out again.

Ludlow's lawyer, Kristen Case, pressed Cho on these physical details.

Q: You passed out again after the cigarette?
A: Yes.
Q: Did you pass out on the floor or in the bed?
A: I don't remember.

If I may be permitted to make Case's implicit point, since nicotine is a stimulant and Cho's last drink had been hours before, passing out drunk *for a second time* at 4:00 a.m. seems physiologically unlikely.

Slavin ruled that Cho was the truthful one.

I find Complainant's testimony that Respondent had his arms around her and that they spooned while sleeping to be credible, especially since Complainant recalled waking up at 4:30 in the morning and having to extricate herself from Respondent's grasp to check her phone. I found Respondent's testimony that they each slept on their own side of the bed with a pillow between them and no physical contact to be unconvincing. Complainant said there was no pillow between them.

The one place Slavin waffled was on whether Ludlow had touched Cho's breasts and buttocks, her most serious charge against him:

Complainant told me she was in and out of consciousness at this time, and in our initial interview, she told me she thought Respondent may have touched her breast and buttock. At her follow-up interview, she said she was pretty sure he had. I find her testimony on this particular point to be fuzzy and, in light of Respondent's denial of touching her breasts and buttocks, I cannot conclude that it is more likely than not that this particular touching occurred.

Then how on earth, not having been in the room herself, can Slavin find that they'd spooned? Can she really make the distinction between spooning and a hand-on-buttock? For those keeping score, it's no to the pillow, yes to Ludlow's arms around Cho and spooning, but no to buttock touching. It's like sexual misconduct roulette.

In the morning, Ludlow drove Cho back to campus. She says that in the car he told her they should see where things went, as far as having a relationship. Ludlow says there was no discussion of a relationship and that they parted on what he thought were normal terms. Back at her dorm, Cho posted a friendly comment on Ludlow's Facebook page about one of the photos he'd taken at one of the galleries, and according to Ludlow, "liked" others, though the next week, she'd say they traumatized her and demand (via Slavin) that Ludlow take them down, which he did.

Then there was the photo Cho herself took of the view from Ludlow's fifty-eighth-floor terrace, which came up at the deposition. "Were you going in and out of consciousness when you took this picture?" Ludlow's lawyer asked.

"I don't remember," Cho replied.

You get the sense that Slavin didn't much like Ludlow—she keeps calling his version of events "self-serving," though what else can someone be when defending himself in a Title IX investigation? The one point on which she found Ludlow more credible than Cho was regarding Cho's claim that Ludlow told her he *loved* her and had asked her to say that she loved him too. Ludlow, Cho claimed, also pointed out that he was in an advantageous position, and could give her anything she wanted if she just asked.

Ludlow denied all this categorically.

Slavin wrote that while she generally found Cho's detailed testimony to be more credible than Ludlow's denials, "I do not find it believable that Respondent told Complainant he loved her." Yet, "I do find that Respondent likely referred to his position, power, contacts, and ability to help Complainant in an effort to get Complainant to spend more time with him or enter into a relationship with him."

At this point I began to suspect that Slavin's relation to Ludlow was as dreamlike as Cho's: there was exactly as much evidence that Ludlow offered to deploy his prestige to help Cho as there was evidence that he told Cho he loved her. If this is how "preponderance" is established, let's just admit it's completely a matter of caprice.

Here's an example of an equally plausible yet more psychologically nuanced story. Perhaps Cho was capable of both flinging herself at Ludlow in a sexualized way and also feeling victimized by him. It wasn't a narrative Slavin entertained, but it wouldn't be an unfamiliar cluster of behaviors to someone working in the mental health sphere. If you describe the sequence of events to a psychiatrist friend, as I did (the flirty emails, the disparate accounts of the evening, Cho's alleged suicide attempt, her professions of PTSD), he might mention that such behaviors are often found in those who've been diagnosed with what's known as "borderline personality disorder," whose themes include both sexual impulsivity and feelings of victimization. On the same diagnostic spectrum, one finds "histrionic personality disorder," whose indicators include provocative or seductive behavior, attention-seeking suicidal gestures or threats, and a tendency for melodrama. I'm not saying such diagnoses apply to Cho. I'm saying they're no less credible as suppositions than the stereotypes about predatory male professors and their helpless female prey that predominate on campus.

Though Slavin declined to scratch many surfaces, a more nuanced portrait of Cho did emerge, under questioning, at her deposition.

At the time of her run-in with Ludlow, her life had not been a particularly easy one. The small restaurant her mother and stepfather ran was struggling, and there were serious financial problems. They were on the verge of declaring bankruptcy, and Cho didn't know where next year's tuition payment would be coming from. She wasn't in touch with her biological father (though she'd lived with him when she was younger), so he was no help. When she'd emailed Ludlow about needing Linden dollars and being "real life broke too," she wasn't exaggerating.

There had been troubles the previous year: an arrest for shoplifting seven hundred dollars' worth of clothes from Macy's, for which she had to pay restitution, and another, smaller-scale shoplifting incident. Maybe this is normal high school stuff, or so Cho said when questioned: "I'm just saying that, you know, it's not habitual behavior. I'm not a criminal. It's just, as you know, teenage girls, like, can make mistakes like that and I have clearly learned my lesson."

Q: How old were you when you shoplifted from Macy's?

A: I was 18.

Q: So you were an adult then, correct?

A: Legally, yes.

The question of Cho's adulthood *was* an implicit element in the case against Ludlow. Adulthood is inconsistently defined, to be sure: at nineteen, Cho was over the age of sexual consent but under legal drinking age. In Slavin's report, Cho is effectively a child; everything happens *to* her. Cho shares the self-conception: adulthood seems to figure as a legal technicality at most. For Ludlow's lawyer, if Cho was over the age of consent then she was a consenting adult. In fact, the question of adulthood—how adult *are* students?—is one of the central issues under renegotiation on campuses at the moment. A previous generation of student activists fought against the *in loco parentis* policies of universities; today's students are fighting to extend them.

Was it fair for Case to bring up the shoplifting arrests in the context of a sexual misconduct inquiry? Or the treacherous, blackmailing previous boyfriend (he'd threatened to tell Cho's employer about the shoplifting episode)? Right-minded people will doubtless say no, given the brutal ways defense attorneys have been allowed to defame accusers in rape trials. Not only shouldn't an accuser's past, sexual or otherwise, be on trial, you also don't have to be a perfect person to be assaulted. With all this, I fully agree. At the same time, if Ludlow's job was on the line based on Cho's credibility, wasn't *some* scrutiny justified?

Not according to the faculty committee who'd later hear the dismissal case against Ludlow, and who declined (as had Slavin) to consider information on Cho's psychological life or history. Nor could the implausibilities in the suicide story be raised. Why? "Survivors must be believed" is the campus mantra.

The problem is the unacknowledged slippage between "survivors" and "accusers." I was rather stunned to receive an email, in March 2014, from the "Title IX Coordinating Committee" on our campus, a group of thirteen administrators tasked with policymaking about sexual misconduct, who were responding to a student petition demanding that "survivors" be informed about the outcomes of sexual harassment investigations. The word *survivor* was repeated eleven times, *in a policy document*, to refer to *accusers*. How can someone be referred to as a survivor *before* a finding on the accusation, assuming we don't want to predetermine the guilt of the accused? I emailed an inquiry to this effect to our university's general counsel, one of the letter's signatories, but got no reply. Another of the signatories was Joan Slavin, who hadn't just investigated Ludlow's case, but—in what's known as the "single investigator model," employed in campus adjudications like these—functioned as both judge and jury.

Why does the use of "survivor" matter? Because language shapes reality. The coordinating committee's haphazard use of it suggests a troubling obliviousness about their roles in shaping the narratives that decide people's fates.

One of the many things I learned from professors who've been the subject of Title IX cases is that there are often shadowy players and issues behind the scenes: departmental rivalries, personal grudges, even scheming exes. It's not unheard of for professors to urge students to press charges against other professors, or otherwise play the process to their advantage. In some cases, an older generation of feminists have proved adept at using vague misconduct allegations to knock off ideological foes, including loathed younger male professors. And what a great opportunity for payback over tenure disputes. (I heard this repeatedly.) Grad students enact Oedipal dramas on their elders and tar sibling competitors with wild accusations. The retaliation factor figures in undergrad student-student cases, too, especially in romances gone wrong. I'm not a big conspiracy theorist, but I've heard this motif repeated often, and seen convincing evidence—given weak evidentiary standards and credulous investigators, the Title IX process is extraordinarily available to manipulation. It's often said that academic politics gets so ugly because the stakes are so low, but the stakes here are people's careers and livelihoods; for students, expulsion and a life derailed.

In Ludlow's situation, I learned—not from him, but from a close reading of the file—that the forces had been marshaling against him long before Cho invited him to that Flux Fest exhibit. Our Title IX officer, Joan Slavin, had known about Ludlow months before hearing about Cho's case. Behind the scenes, other stories were playing out that infused Cho's with even greater potency. I'll get to more of the particulars shortly, but for now, let's talk about the sex lives of avatars.

Remember that student journalist who'd visited Ludlow's Philosophy of Cyberspace class? He'd clearly been well schooled in the art of a punchy lede, opening his article with a tableau of bored students browsing online Banana Republic catalogues and checking their Gmail—that is, until Ludlow began projecting clips of avatars having sex: ". . . fantastical, multicolored creatures with tails and wings writhe on huge, ornate digital beds. Masochism, sadism, whips, and bondage flash across the screen. The video culminates with what appears to be a demon fem-bot urinating on her sexual partner—a virtual golden shower." Adds the journalist, "No one is looking for fall wardrobe staples anymore."

In film theory (closer to my area), the juxtaposition of two shots is called *montage*. Even when shots are taken at different times and places, placing one shot in juxtaposition to the next creates a connection—this is the fundamental principle of film editing. The great Russian filmmaker Serge Eisenstein elaborated on the implications in his theory of "dialectical montage," which means, basically, that abutting two unrelated shots creates a new meaning, a synthesis, that neither originally had on its own. The second shot changes the meaning of the first; the first informs the second.

So, too, with paragraphs. Now let's transpose montage theory to departmental politics, since it helps explain what happened next. The student journalist followed the fem-bot paragraph with a quote from the chair of the philosophy department, who said: "When you think of a philosophy professor . . . you often think of someone who sits in his or her chair in the office thinking and not doing very much—that does not describe Ludlow at all."

Abutting the philosophy chair's comment about Ludlow, and the paragraph about the avatars having sex, created the effect that the chair was commenting approvingly on Ludlow's choice of visual examples, even though the chair apparently knew nothing about the avatars until the article was published. His response was not a happy one. He burst into Ludlow's office, according to Ludlow, "and started screaming obscenities like 'What the fuck, what the fuck!'" In fact, he was so unhappy that he headed straight to the dean's office to discuss the matter.

His ire not exhausted, he paid a visit to Joan Slavin, our Title IX officer, to confer with her about the pornographic avatars, and while they were conferring, he brought up *other* concerns about Ludlow's conduct, including rumors he'd heard about his behavior at a conference in South America two years before. Also, there were rumors that Ludlow seemed quite "close" to two female grad students in the philosophy program.

Slavin set about trying to confirm these rumors and dig up information on Ludlow—even though there had been no official complaint from anyone. She asked Ludlow's colleague who'd brought the rumors to the chair to meet with her. The colleague declined, saying that what she'd heard was hearsay, though she'd later become a prime behind-the-scenes mover in Ludlow's dismissal case.

After Cho made her allegations, Slavin contacted the two grad students whose names the chair had given her. One refused to return Slavin's calls, despite pressure from the chair. The other came in for a meeting, but said she didn't want to get involved. We'll be hearing more about this meeting later.

In short, by the time Cho and Ludlow were walking to his car that February afternoon, Slavin had already been investigating Ludlow for some time. The accusation machinery was up and running.

And why *did* the chair get so exercised about Ludlow showing clips of pornographic avatars? The avatars didn't even resemble humans—"It was a robot and a furry," Ludlow said, laughing. (For those not up on their fantasy fan subcultures, "furries" are human-size stuffed animals with human personalities and characteristics. Sometimes people dressed in furry costumes meet up at furry conventions to socialize and "scritch" each other—light scratching and grooming—and to hook up with other furries.) The fact is that Ludlow had solid pedagogical reasons for showing the clip, which was part of a lecture on the changing culture of *Second Life*. The once-innovative virtual world had gone from a creative platform with a subcultural prankster ethos to an increasingly corporate environment: avatars in virtual neckties sitting around virtual mahogany tables. Even IBM had been producing such content, which Ludlow was contrasting with the revelry of the pissing avatars. He'd prepared a twenty-eight-part PowerPoint to accompany the lecture, and had dutifully issued a trigger warning.

He didn't know the chair had gone to Slavin about the avatars until he read Slavin's Title IX report. He'd been angry when she brought up the avatars in her interview with him, thinking it violated his academic freedom. As with the creative writing teacher forced to defend Whitman, Title IX officers who know nothing about the relevant subjects seem rather too willing to pounce on hints of sexuality in the curriculum. (In fact, professors in colleges and universities around the country have been teaching courses on pornography for the last twenty-five years, and there are hundreds of dissertations and scholarly articles on the subjects.)

"Why *did* the chair turn on you?" I asked Ludlow. A chair reporting a professor in his department to a Title IX officer struck me as a pretty radical step. He said he didn't know.

"Were you an outsider?" I pressed. I was thinking that in Salem a number of the accused witches were on the periphery of the community, or so historian John Demos argues in *Entertaining Satan*, an analysis of the cultural context of the witch trials.

"I don't know. I think it's possible I was so much of an outsider I didn't know there was an inside and an outside."

This turned out to be true. In fact, the more I dug into the situation, and people started passing information my way, the more convoluted Ludlow's case came to seem. There were various competing agendas, not to mention toxic levels of self-exoneration and scapegoating. There were known "climate issues" in the department (philosophy departments nationwide are rife with harassment issues), and some ugly behavior, including by one or two male graduate students, who would, along with assorted interlopers, attempt to involve themselves in the case against Ludlow. Ludlow himself hadn't even known the full extent of the backstage machinations.

In case I haven't made it sufficiently clear, I absolutely believe there are sexual harassers on campus, and bona fide harassers should be fired. Then there's bona fide sexual hysteria, the fantasy that predators are lurking around every corner. In fact, having been a little ironic about campus dangers turned me into one of these fantasy figures myself.

Following the campus protests over my sexual paranoia essay, I'd finally weaned myself away from the online coverage when someone kindly alerted me to an article by a young feminist professor at another college comparing me to Hannibal Lecter. I tried to ignore this information, but ended up clicking on the link anyway. The piece was endless, but the gist seemed to be that I was *cannibalizing* students by writing about them. The article was illustrated with a creepy photo of the television Hannibal fondling a skull. I confess that being compared to a charismatic fictional serial killer wasn't entirely unflattering, given the glamour and esteem popular culture accords such figures at the moment, but still, it was a little weird.

I suddenly recalled that I'd once *met* the author of the cannibal accusation: she showed up with someone at a book party I'd thrown for my boyfriend a few years before, and we were introduced. Playing the hostess, I'd been circulating among the guests with little quiches on a platter and offered her one. Not her own brains fricasseed and served *en croute* or other diabolical Lecter-ish specialties, but a mini-quiche lovingly defrosted and baked with my own hands. I can't recall if she took it, but on consideration, the memory of my gracious hospitality made the cannibalism reproach seem all the more daft—though not so different in degree from the projections and hyperbolic fantasies lately dominating campus culture.

Still, I was also aware that my accuser was someone in a more precarious professional situation than mine, and wondered to what extent displaced career and economic anxieties are contributing factors in these intergenerational fantasies of predation.

There's a reality to academic privilege—old people have the few remaining good jobs, we're not ready to give them up, and a lot of younger people feel eaten alive in the academic marketplace, which is more brutal these days than ever. But casting real people in fictive roles isn't a harmless pastime. I can joke about being turned into a charismatic predator for writing an essay, but it's a luxury not afforded everyone—male professors who become the object of someone's fantasies are likely to end up jobless and destitute.

John Demos notes in *Entertaining Satan*, "As anthropologists have observed in cultures around the world, people who think themselves bewitched are vulnerable to all manner of mischance. They blunder into 'accidents'; they lose their effectiveness in work and social relations; at least occasionally they sicken and die." Such was the case with Ludlow's accuser Eunice Cho, who testified that she'd suffered all these fates after the forced drinking session. As history tells us, adds Demos, the imperiled not infrequently become perilous themselves. Thus are communities justified in casting out demons, the ones they'd needed to create.

Which was Ludlow's designated role in the story. "Every culture has its whirlpools of callousness, of cruelty," says Demos, though he's also curious about whether any of the accused Salem witches may have helped incite the charges against them. "Was there also some veiled complicity" he asks, "such as one often finds in habitual victims?" In other words, what sorts of characters find themselves caught up in witch hunts? Who manages to evade scrutiny?

Having been a Title IX respondent myself, it seems like a question worth asking—it's something one would want to know about oneself.

Let me be honest: you're not going to find me arguing that Ludlow showed fantastic judgment in inviting Cho into his apartment, or buying her drinks. Neither would have been unusual when I was in school; now they're signs of degeneracy. It's the new reality, and it behooves us social citizens to occasionally curtsey to the reality principle, at least in public. But I don't know what happened between Cho and Ludlow that night any more than Joan Slavin does, and another principle worth upholding is the one about people being innocent until proved guilty, at least in this country. Absent Slavin's prejudices about male behavior, there simply isn't a preponderance of evidence supporting Cho's story.

Let's say, just as a thought experiment, that Cho came on to Ludlow, and he told her to chill—that he was willing to spend an evening having drinks and going to galleries, but had no interest in taking it further. Is it inconceivable that a professionally ambitious young woman, after spending months emailing her famous professor about this and that, finds herself in his company and decides to test the waters? Let's go further: if we're cynical enough to think Ludlow offered to promote Cho's career in exchange for sex or romance, why aren't we cynical enough to think that Cho spotted a potential gravy train and decided to play it for what she could get? After all, the gold digger and the predatory professor inhabit the same universe of crude stereotypes.

None of which makes Ludlow's judgment any better. When I asked him what on earth he'd been thinking, he replied, "Well, it was 2012." I'm all too aware that to gloat, "He should have seen it coming," coasts on an unseemly admix of hindsight and self-congratulation: "*I'd* never be that stupid," we tell ourselves. But he *was* fatally unobservant: ignoring the tectonic cultural shifts that had been rattling American campuses for quite a while, even if they hadn't yet been completely formalized that snowy February evening.

All of which complicated my own relation to him—like Slavin, I, too, felt a need to castigate him. In Cho's account, Ludlow remarks at one point that when women pass a certain age, "it's almost like they become, like, so mentally rigid or something." Ludlow says he never said it, but isn't this the repertoire of the wised-up middle-aged man rather than a nineteen-year-old girl? When I brought this up to him, with perhaps a bit of an edge— whether at the alleged remark or the condition being invoked, I can't really say—he looked abashed and said he'd recently been dating an "age-appropriate" woman who barely wanted to leave the house. His social world had shrunk to the size of a postage stamp.

I recognized myself in that description: I, too, leave the house only under duress. If I were a middle-aged male professor, would I find hanging out with energetic undergrads an alluring prospect? In my way, I'm probably as much of an institutional rebel as Ludlow, so why is it that my vanity wouldn't be stoked by the attentions of a student, even a smart, attractive one? It's not that I don't occasionally find students sexy or charming. I'm not dead. I'm not even particularly virtuous. I'm curious to find that I don't have a very good way of answering this question.

Still, I understood what Ludlow meant about it having been 2012. At some point in the last five or ten years, sexual suspicion overtook campus; drinking and socializing with undergrads became criminal, even when technically permitted, even if professors and students drinking together (from post-seminar beers to Oxbridge sherry) has been a long-standing custom. A male professor who'd gone through his own Title IX ordeal told me that even meeting a student off campus for coffee had been regarded by his interrogators as criminal.

Ludlow was oddly trusting: he somehow thought that if the rules said you could date students you weren't grading, then you could spend an evening socializing with an undergrad. (It was a "working evening" he said.) At most, he paid for Cho's drinks despite her being underage, a technicality in his eyes. "No one was out doing mudslides or kamikazes," he said. This too turned out to be naïve—buying Cho liquor was regarded as the equivalent of pushing heroin on her. In Joan Slavin's slippery-slope evidentiary standards, if he'd paid for drinks, it meant he'd groped Cho; if he was male, he came on to her.

And that's all it takes to establish a preponderance of evidence under Title IX. I recently read a description of the Saudi legal system: "Justice is often situational; the law is what a person in a position of power decides it is." It sounded uncomfortably close to life on American campuses at the moment.

The university steered a middle course in response to Slavin's report, perhaps because Slavin herself found Cho's testimony "fuzzy" on the breast and buttock touching; perhaps because university higher-ups were aware that Slavin's report was itself, in key respects, fuzzy.

Whatever precise calculations happened behind the scenes, the termination process was not launched. Dismissing a tenured professor at our university requires an elaborate process involving multiple procedures and reports, beginning with the convening of the Masonic-sounding "Committee on Cause." That would come later. Instead, a range of not insubstantial penalties were imposed: Ludlow was stripped of his named chair, his salary was cut, he was required to complete a harassment prevention training program. There was also a no-contact directive, assuming he'd want to contact Cho, which seemed unlikely.

For Cho, this was way too mild. She wanted Ludlow fired. She'd claim, in her lawsuit against the university, that she ran into him constantly on campus and that every time she saw him (or any balding man, or an Audi) it triggered her PTSD, to the point of causing her to pass out. What a powerfully dangerous man he was, to have such magical effects! She emailed various administrators to inform them of these encounters and the emotional toll they took—she'd once even been forced to ride an elevator with him! (Ludlow says he never rode an elevator with Cho and wasn't on campus any of the dates she said she'd seen him.)

Cho retold the story of her February evening with Ludlow to a succession of professors (at least five), typically to explain why she was late with assignments or absent from class. Based on her PTSD, she asked for and got various accommodations from the university disability office: incompletes in classes, flexibility in attendance and assignment due dates, and an assigned note taker. (Queried by Ludlow's lawyer about why she needed a note taker, usually provided for students with hearing or physical disabilities, Cho said it was because she couldn't focus.) These accommodations went on for three years. The university was also paying her medical bills. Cho requested a single room—when Ludlow's lawyer asked if this was because she hadn't gotten along with her roommate freshman year, Cho acknowledged that the roommate had been a "pretentious prick," but that that hadn't been the reason.

If victim status has become a form of cultural capital on campus, Cho was definitely getting the princess treatment.

A year or so after Slavin's report, one of Cho's professors (someone I'm friendly with, though we agree to disagree on many things) encouraged Cho to file a police report about Ludlow, and accompanied her to a Chicago police station to make a statement. This time around, Cho said that Ludlow had been angry and threatening to her during the evening in question and had physically pushed her onto the elevator in his building, though at the deposition she'd say she didn't remember if any of this happened. In the police report, she says she woke up in Ludlow's bed to find him trying to remove her clothes and groping her under her garments. She pleaded, "Please don't rape me"—though she'd said none of this to Slavin. The police concluded that there wasn't enough evidence to proceed with a case, though my professor pal told the campus paper that Cho had been very convincing and that the police had clearly believed her. (Ludlow was never contacted by the police, according to his lawyer.)

The discrepancies among her various accounts would later emerge as an issue for Cho.

Once Cho's lawsuits against Ludlow and the university went public, so did the details of Slavin's damning report, which somehow found their way into our student paper and the local media. One suspects someone thought this would help pave the way for a settlement. Ludlow could no longer set foot in a classroom, though a planned sit-in of one of his courses had to be quickly rethought when he preemptively canceled class. Instead, a hundred or so students, mouths taped shut (by themselves), marched to the dean's office to protest Ludlow's continued presence on campus. The university asked him not to teach the following quarter, though he'd continue to be paid. The local media called him a rapist; Ludlow sued for defamation. A judge ruled that the difference between sexual assault and rape was immaterial, though even Slavin hadn't concluded he'd sexually assaulted Cho. "Unwelcome and inappropriate sexual advances" was as far as she went.

Cho entered campus mythology as a survivor, a plucky heroine standing up to the university's indifference, just as she'd stood up to the sexual predator who'd tried to have his way with her. Ludlow entered campus mythology as a demon. Such are the pre-assigned roles and predetermined pieties of our time.

For my part, I could only see Cho as the unlucky product of a system devoted to persuading a generation of young women that they're helpless prey. Unfortunate enough to have her story of violated femininity enforced by officialdom, Cho was interred in the same aggrieved passivity that entrapped females worldwide have perfected over the centuries. It's a disheartening spectacle—wasn't all this supposed to be behind us already?

2

Flip-Flopping on Consent

A "YES" BECOMES A "NO" YEARS AFTER THE FACT

Sexual consent can now be retroactively withdrawn (with official sanction) years later, based on changing feelings or residual ambivalence, or new circumstances. Please note that this makes anyone who's ever had sex a potential rapist.

In February 2014, shortly after Eunice Cho's allegations against Peter Ludlow were made public, a philosophy grad student named Nola Hartley and a philosophy professor named Jocelyn Packer had a discussion about Ludlow while the two were at an academic conference.[*] Packer was Hartley's thesis advisor; she was also the colleague of Ludlow's who, back in the fall of 2011, approached the philosophy department chair with her suspicions about Ludlow, which he'd relayed to Joan Slavin.

The odd thing is that Packer and Ludlow had once been friendly, or close enough that when his then-teenage daughter was visiting, they had dinner with Packer and her family. Ludlow thinks the friendship may have gone downhill after a spat about a hiring decision—Ludlow hadn't supported Packer's can-

---

[*] Both women's names are pseudonyms.

didate, who didn't get the job. Packer would later complain to Joan Slavin that Ludlow had girlfriends half his age and poor moral judgment, so maybe the estrangement had nothing to do with turf wars—but who knows? My question is whether the moral judgment of the moral judges is all that reliable either. I'm not sure it was in this case.

Apparently distraught over the revelations in Cho's lawsuit, Hartley told Packer that Eunice Cho's complaint against Ludlow was "similar" to what had happened to her two and a half years earlier: Ludlow had courted her by expressing interest in her work, flattering her intellect, and inviting her to co-write an article with him. They'd ended up having what she now described as an "inappropriate professor/student relationship."

Consensual relationships between professors and grad students weren't against university policy (and still aren't), as long as the professor isn't in a supervisory position, and Ludlow had never been Nola Hartley's professor or advisor. Hartley was twenty-five at the time, obviously well over the age of consent. Whether Ludlow had been in a supervisory position became one of the points of contention in their respective stories, and one of the many things Hartley changed her mind about.

Hartley and Ludlow had indeed had a relationship, and it was, at the time, consensual. This is well documented, since the two were in constant online contact during the three or so months they were involved: particularly in the early, heady days of the romance, there were as many as eighty texts in a single day. There are mutual professions of love, and trading of pet names—she called him "1000 angels" (a *30 Rock* reference), and made it his nickname on her phone—though she'd later say it meant nothing. There were frequent exchanges about domestic and social arrangements (they were spending most nights together), the sharing of departmental gossip, philosophical ruminations, and household minutiae (she: "Why did you buy rice milk *and* soy milk?"). They also had a mutual interest in the nerdier corners of online fandom, such as the *My Little Pony: Friendship Is Magic* cult, based on the animated TV show. An early exchange discusses crashing a "brony" party at Northwestern—male *My Little Pony* fans, known as "bronies," revere, and occasionally dress as, prancing rainbow-colored ponies; they greet one another by "bro-hoofing," a term that comes up not infrequently in Ludlow and Hartley's exchanges.

Between emails, texts, Gchat, and Facebook, there are well over two thousand discrete messages. There may be no better-documented relationship in the history of humanity.

I know all this because I've digested the entirety. When I interviewed Ludlow in Mexico, he allowed me to read through it all, from which I learned that Hartley had keys to Ludlow's apartment, drove his car, and stayed at his place when he was out of town. They discussed her meeting his daughter. Hartley wrote proposing future outings; he proposed a trip to Rome. They talked about redecorating his apartment. At one point he texts that he'd put her down as an emergency contact during a doctor's appointment, and she writes back that she'd been thinking that very day of making him hers.

During our interview, Ludlow tried to interest me in *My Little Pony*, too, insisting at one point that I watch a video clip of a bunch of winsome animated ponies cavorting in a candy-colored field, which was the longest three minutes of my life. I got the sense that despite everything, part of him was nostalgic for what he and Hartley had shared. With this I could empathize: I know from experience that once you've emotionally attached yourself, unattaching (even from someone who's acted monstrously) can take years.

But everything I learned about this relationship—and I learned *a lot*—also throws into question all easy assumptions about institutional roles alone determining who has more power in romantic entanglements. For instance, it's a well-known fact that if you're in two relationships simultaneously, as Hartley was—she had another boyfriend, who lived in Boston—you alter the balance of power in your favor. It's a well-known fact that whoever's more in love has less power. Youth and attractiveness may also offset the weight of institutional standing and higher degrees; so do calculations about who's more likely to end things first, as Hartley eventually did, ditching Ludlow for the out-of-town boyfriend, whom she'd later marry. This prior boyfriend's existence had become a source of tension between her and Ludlow in the end stages of their own relationship, as Ludlow pressed for more of a commitment, which is never a pretty position to find yourself in, especially when it comes to preserving an equal balance of power between two people.

Curiously, despite being in another relationship herself, when Hartley and Ludlow were first getting together she asked him to stop seeing a woman *he'd* been casually involved with—Hartley sent texts to this effect—which bespeaks a certain confidence in itself. Ludlow was single and dating various women at the time. (He'd been married for ten years to a professor at his previous university, but they'd divorced long before he came to Northwestern in 2008.) In my understanding of human affairs, it seems clear that if Hartley asked Ludlow to break things off with another woman, then her later claims about their relationship—

that she'd never been romantic about him, that she'd thought of him strictly as a mentor—were either untrue or pretty radical revisions of what had actually taken place.

The question becomes how seriously we, and the campus officials who adjudicate the sorts of charges Hartley would later bring, should take a retrospective retraction of consent to a relationship by one of the parties two years later. (What would it mean to not consent to sending *a thousand texts and emails?*) Let me add that the consent-retraction isn't an issue in this case alone. It features in many others around the country, usually against male students who find out weeks, months, or years after the fact that sexual encounters they'd thought were consensual (including specific acts in the context of ongoing relationships) have been reassessed by the other person as having been coerced or otherwise nonconsensual.

One problem with these retroactive accusations is that memory doesn't exactly sharpen over time. In fact, most memory research demonstrates that subsequent events reshape and distort our memories, and the more we recall a given memory, the less accurate it becomes. These revisions accumulate, and can come to seem just as "true" as what actually happened.

The license to rewrite consent also requires a lot of historical amnesia about women's struggles to shed the constricting innocence patriarchy once imposed on us, namely, the sexual double standard. Sure, sexual freedom sometimes means consenting to things we later regret. But who wants a return to nineteenth-century notions of true womanhood, which conferred moral superiority on females by exempting them from such corruptions and temptations, placing them on a pedestal they finally (thankfully) refused. The pedestal was always a lie, and its twenty-first-century resurrection on campus is no less a lie. Sexual honesty, about women as desiring beings, making our own sexual choices (sometimes even terrible ones), can be painful, but no semblance of gender equality is ever going to be possible without it.

Several weeks after the conversation between Nola Hartley and her advisor (and over two years after the events in question), Hartley dropped a new bombshell. Hysterical and crying, she revealed to Jocelyn Packer that Ludlow had once had sex with her without her consent when she was drunk. They'd been drinking at his place, and the next thing she remembered was waking up in his bed in the morning naked and realizing what had happened. They'd had sex one additional time, she confessed, while they were both again drunk, though this time it was consensual. They'd only had sex those two times, she said.

Ludlow would later say that he and Hartley had sex regularly for three months and it had always been consensual. He also said it under oath when deposed in the Cho case. Hartley has never been deposed or given any statements under oath.

Packer immediately contacted Joan Slavin. (As a graduate advisor, Packer was what's known as a "mandatory reporter," that is, required to report any sexual assault information that came her way.) Slavin emailed Hartley asking if she was willing to talk. Hartley emailed back saying that she was afraid to talk to anyone on campus because "Ludlow was too powerful."

What's curious about this chronology, which is repeated in the eventual Title IX report, is that Hartley knew about Eunice Cho's complaints against Ludlow long before she confessed her own relationship with him to her advisor. Joan Slavin had disclosed the gist to Hartley two years earlier, during the Cho investigation—Hartley was one of the two grad students whose names the philosophy chair had turned over to Slavin in fall 2011. Likewise, the news about Nola Hartley and Ludlow couldn't have come as much of a surprise to Professor Packer: she herself had reported rumors about them to the chair. When Slavin had attempted to get Hartley to discuss her relationship with Ludlow (in February 2012), they'd met, and though Hartley spoke harshly of him—this was shortly after their breakup—she declined to participate in the Cho investigation, telling Slavin that while her relationship with Ludlow hadn't been "altogether pleasant," it didn't mirror what she knew of Cho's situation. All this is recorded in Slavin's notes about the conversation.*

Having read through these notes, and the rest of the documents that accumulated in the case, so many discrepancies leap out that it's impossible to know where to start. To begin with: if Ludlow had raped Hartley a month or two before Hartley was informed by Slavin that Eunice Cho had filed a sexual assault charge against him, why would she have told Slavin, at the time, that the two situations were dissimilar?

One possible answer: in the aftermath of their relationship, Hartley may have been on the outs with Ludlow, but the idea

---

* The university treated Ludlow's eventual dismissal hearing like a mini-trial, providing him with all the background documents from both investigations, as would have happened during the discovery process in a civil case. Ludlow referred to it as a document dump, but I was never sure whether the university was being strategic, or attempting to be transparent.

that he'd raped her only came later. Clearly the idea that the relationship itself had been nonconsensual came later, as Hartley herself told the Title IX investigator assigned to the case. "It wasn't until years later that she'd started to get some perspective on what happened, by opening up to friends and advisors about it," the investigator records, scribbling in her notes, "KEY!!"

Though the investigator was supposed to be neutral, there were a lot of celebratory exclamation points in the notes, apparently at moments when she felt she'd nabbed her man.

Based on the information Professor Packer had provided, Joan Slavin contacted the university's general counsel. Since Slavin was named in Eunice Cho's lawsuit against Northwestern over what Cho maintained had been insufficiently tough penalties imposed on Ludlow, the decision was made to hire an outsider to conduct the new Title IX investigation. A Chicago lawyer named Patricia Bobb, a former assistant state's attorney now in private practice, was chosen for the task.

It was a curious choice, since Bobb had no previous experience with Title IX investigations. Her résumé is long on personal injury litigation and medical malpractice, including numerous citations from the 1980s (in *Time, Glamour, Town & Country*) lauding her as an outstanding female trial lawyer and "working woman." She may well be all those things, but for an academic (even a quasi-academic like me), reading Bobb's report brings to mind an amateur anthropologist who's dropped in to study the natives and keeps mistaking funerals for puberty rites, and vice versa. Her lack of experience with academic culture leads her to cast the most routine interactions in a nefarious light, while overlooking numerous glaring contradictions in the narrative she seems determined to tell.

After some hesitation, Hartley agreed to meet with Bobb, despite her professed fear of Ludlow. Packer and Slavin were apparently both urging her on, though Hartley had also contacted a feminist philosophy professor at Southern Connecticut State University named Heidi Lockwood, who advised Hartley not to go into a meeting without a lawyer. We'll be hearing more about Lockwood, a self-styled carpetbagging rape activist with a propensity for inserting herself into sexual misconduct cases, and who became Hartley's backstage advisor in this one. Bobb wouldn't allow Hartley to bring a lawyer, though eventually Hartley came around, having decided that speaking out against Ludlow was her moral obligation.

Hartley was extremely emotional and cried through the majority of their three-hour conversation, Bobb reports. Jocelyn Packer came along as a support person. Hartley repeated the story she'd told Packer: she'd woken up in Ludlow's bed wearing no underwear and realized they'd had sex without her consent after too much wine the evening before, though she didn't actually remember anything about the sex.

When Bobb eventually contacted Ludlow to tell him that he was the subject of new complaints, he wasn't surprised: rumors had been raging in the philosophy community for weeks, and even mentioned on the professional blogs, that new charges were pending. Hartley's confidants hadn't exactly been discreet. Ludlow had first gotten word from a woman philosopher friend at another school who said she'd heard it from Heidi Lockwood, who'd been calling people with the news.

Ludlow's meeting with Bobb lasted more than four hours. She told him she was investigating a report of "an inappropriate relationship" between him and a grad student, and an allegation of nonconsensual sex. Though the nonconsensual sex accusation was a potentially criminal matter, Bobb told him he was allowed only "a support person," no lawyer. Ludlow was thus forced into a four-hour meeting with a former Chicago prosecutor, and anything he said could have been used against him in an eventual prosecution. Nevertheless, he came alone—he had no choice—prepared to defend himself against the sex allegation, but soon realized Bobb was investigating the entire relationship, despite there being no university code against such relationships.

Being investigated for something there's no rule against probably sounds strange to anyone who hasn't spent the last year hearing about the cases of professors and students in precisely the same predicament, but not much would surprise me at this point on the due process front.

Ludlow had put together a binder with a time line of his three-month relationship with Hartley, transcripts of their online correspondence, and photos of Hartley in his apartment, all of which made it abundantly clear there'd been a consensual romance. Starting in early October of that year, Hartley regularly slept over, and frequently told him she loved him, he told Bobb (evidence: dozens of texts). They'd spent more evenings together than apart when both were in town, often going out to dinner and concerts (evidence: excited texts from Hartley about getting to see Jay Z and Kanye West). He thought they cared deeply for each other (evidence: numerous texts to that effect). He'd been in love with her; they'd fantasized about a life together (evidence: texts about décor for a future country home—steampunk). But in the end, Hartley had decided to work things out with her previous boyfriend. He'd hoped to stay friends.

He denied the nonconsensual sex charge. He also didn't understand why she'd continue to be loving and friendly toward him through December, stay over at his place (evidence: more texts), and even travel to an out-of-town concert (Bon Iver) and stay in a hotel room together if, as she was now saying, he'd raped her in November.

It also turned out that Ludlow had a hotel receipt for the November night Hartley claimed the rape took place (copy provided): it happened to be the night before both were leaving town for Thanksgiving break. They'd had an argument about her not being able to choose between Ludlow and the Boston boyfriend, who'd recently been visiting: Ludlow had felt wounded when Hartley completely dropped out of touch, which left him feeling emotionally exposed, and reevaluating their relationship. Hartley had told Ludlow the other relationship was rocky—she couldn't talk about her work, communication was bad. Ludlow thought for a while that she was close to ending it, but that wasn't happening. He accused her of choosing by not choosing. After the fight, he went to stay at a hotel a few blocks away. When I asked him why, he said sheepishly that it's his habit to check into a hotel when things get emotionally tense.

Ludlow also supplied Bobb with texts from the morning after the alleged rape—Hartley was still at his place, and left from there for the airport. The texts say nothing about nonconsensual sex. Instead, they're about Ludlow having decided to break things off the night before—he'd been worried Hartley was going to reunite with her boyfriend over the break and wanted to get out before that happened. *"I just can't bear the pain of trying to play it cool while u are with _____ trying to work things out,"* he wrote. She asks if she can still tell him she loves him. He responds, *"Dude, I don't know. It fucks up my head. I wanted to marry you and spend the rest of my life with you. I don't know."*

What jumped out at me in these texts—the morning after the alleged rape—is that it's Hartley who's repeatedly apologizing for hurting *Ludlow* by vacillating between him and the other boyfriend. Two years later, the axis of injury would be flipped: now the story is that Ludlow had hurt *her*, that *he'd* been the injurious one.

Except that the texts themselves say otherwise:

> HARTLEY: "I don't want to hurt anybody. I just don't know what I want."
> HARTLEY: "I can't even begin to apologize for hurting you."
> HARTLEY: "As in all things shitty, this too shall pass. I love you."

Ludlow's fears that he was about to be dumped were temporarily allayed when Hartley returned from Thanksgiving break and the two continued seeing each other for a few more weeks. In fact, Hartley *did* finally break up with the Boston boyfriend in early December, though this turned out to be short-lived—she confessed her relationship with Ludlow to him over Christmas break, then told Ludlow that things were over when he picked her up in a cab at the airport in early January.

So how did Patricia Bobb, first-time Title IX investigator, build her case against Ludlow? We saw Joan Slavin deploying tired biases about male and female nature in the first investigation, and renaming them "preponderance of evidence." With such biases now firmly installed as campus policy (minus any public scrutiny or discussion, needless to say), the case hardly needed to be built: stereotypes about predatory male sexuality and the eternal innocence of women will suffice.

After her meeting with Ludlow, Bobb forwarded copies of the texts and emails Ludlow had given her to Nola Hartley, at which point Hartley altered her story: she confirmed that they'd had "what became a romantic relationship." Yes, Hartley now conceded, she'd spent many nights at Ludlow's place and slept with him, but she'd *worn clothes to bed.* They had consensual sex, *but only once.* When she'd said she loved Ludlow, she meant it *at the time.* And maybe the rape *didn't* actually take place the night before they left town for Thanksgiving; maybe it had been sometime in December?

Ludlow says they both slept naked, so Hartley waking up naked wouldn't have been out of the ordinary. Among the photographs he supplied Bobb was one of Hartley in a bathrobe at his apartment—she's bare-legged and doesn't appear to be clothed underneath. Another artier photo shows a shadow of what looks like a nude Hartley on the wall.

The question becomes why Bobb would ultimately favor Hartley's new account of the relationship over Ludlow's account, which was backed by numerous forms of evidence, both textual and photographic. In Bobb's handwritten notes, the sections about Ludlow are scattered with comments such as *"don't believe," "makes no sense," "wrong,"* and *"bullshit."* When Ludlow speaks about his feelings, Bobb scrawls *"manipulative."*

She doesn't just disbelieve Ludlow; she ignores key pieces of evidence he provides about the relationship. There was the question of who initiated things, which Bobb makes much of, writing falsely, "It is uncontested that Ludlow invited Complainant to lunch after she attended one of his lectures in the early fall of 2011." According to Bobb, Hartley was walking out of Ludlow's class after a lecture (except that she never *took* a class with him), and Ludlow approached her and invited her to lunch. "The Complainant was flattered by Ludlow's attention, his interest in her intellectual ability and his offer to work with her on philosophy. . . . She was lonely and eager to work with him and be his friend."

Except there are Facebook messages showing that Hartley and another grad student in the department were the ones who invited Ludlow to lunch. They'd all been at another philosophy professor's apartment in the city for drinks; at the end of the evening, Ludlow gave the two women cab fare so they wouldn't have to take public transportation home. A few days later the friend Facebook messaged, "Dude, peter—you gave us way too much $$ for the taxi." Hartley chimes in: "We're taking you to lunch. Deal with it."

Ludlow texts Hartley later that evening: "Are we doing lunch tomorrow?"

Hartley, a minute later: "YES. Man, if you wanted to do 'lunch' right now I'd say yes. Anything to distract me from moral disagreement."

Ludlow: "Wtf? Are u reading that crap for [Packer's] class?"

Hartley: "Dude, it's fucking painful. I'm reading a paper entitled 'On blanket statements about the epistemic effects of religious diversity.' Kill me."

Ludlow showed up for lunch thinking both Hartley and her friend would be there. Hartley showed up alone.

Bobb's version:

Clearly it was Ludlow's intention at this point early in their re-
lationship to engage Complainant in a personal and potentially
romantic relationship. In fact, this lunch marks the beginning of
Ludlow's socializing with Complainant outside of school. Ludlow
admits that during the rest of their relationship, they often drank
wine when they were together.

Among the many points Bobb seems determined to miss are
that Ludlow didn't initiate lunch, and that Hartley was neither
lonely nor particularly awed by him. (Also that grad students and
faculty not infrequently drink together.) What Bobb especially
ignores is that Hartley would appear to be flirting with Ludlow
(note the flirty quotes around "lunch"), which would have gotten
in the way of Bobb's determination that desire can be only a one-
way street, and that Ludlow alone is driving the bus. "I do not
believe that Complainant was the aggressor as their social relationship developed," writes Bobb. "Given her age and the imbal-
ance of power between then, she was vulnerable and susceptible
to his conduct." Hartley was, as mentioned, twenty-five.

Speaking of power . . . Let's be honest. It's a well-known (if,
to some, unpalatable) fact that heterosexual women are not infrequently attracted to male power, and for aspiring female in-
tellectuals of a heterosexual bent, this includes male intellectual
power. Even feminists (feminist philosophers included) aren't
immune. What use to anyone is a feminism so steeped in self-
exoneration that it prefers to imagine women as helpless children
rather than acknowledge grown-up sexual realities?

The omissions and misreadings continue through the report,

with Bobb, like a bad novelist armed with a repertoire of stock characters, transforming Hartley at every opportunity from an active agent into a childlike waif. In lieu of a woman with a master's degree in philosophy, Bobb gives us a Dickensian urchin. Take her tale of Hartley's penurious grad school existence— the broken futon, the tiny room ("What grad student doesn't live that way?" Ludlow pointed out)—which accounts for why Hartley keeps finding herself, *accidentally*, spending the night at Ludlow's:

Bobb (paraphrasing Hartley):

The Complainant did not have much money, and Ludlow bought her drinks and meals at expensive restaurants in the city. They spent hours having philosophical discussions, some of which took place at his apartment in the city. At the time, the Complainant was living in a single room with a futon for a bed and had virtually no money. . . . She sometimes stayed at his apartment in the city after a late night with him when she did not want to have to go back north to her apartment closer to campus.

Among the problems with this account is that Hartley didn't end up staying at Ludlow's accidentally, because she didn't want to make the journey home. She purposefully left home *to go to* Ludlow's, frequently at ten or eleven at night, as the correspondence makes perfectly clear.

Bobb (paraphrasing Hartley):

She was lonely and eager to work with him and be his friend. . . . She began to sleep at his apartment in his bed, but she remained

clothed and they did not have sex. Ludlow was increasingly pres-
suring her to take their relationship to a new level, which she knew
meant having sex.

Except that Bobb had *seen* the bathrobed photo of Hartley at Ludlow's place, except that Hartley's social life was a whirl of friends and outings, except that the texts show that work was one subject among many. As far as sexual pressure, there were back-and-forth texts like these:

LUDLOW: "There is a red hair on the pillow next to me. I miss."
HARTLEY: "I seriously just said 'awwww' out loud."
LUDLOW: "I am seriously hearing you snort as you read this."

According to Bobb's report:

Throughout the relationship, the Complainant was conflicted. She
was close to Ludlow and depended on him. They were affectionate
with each other and she wanted him to be happy. She loved him as
a friend, but was never in love with him.

Except there are dozens of texts saying the opposite:

HARTLEY (AT 11:00 p.m.): "If I could I would teleport there right
   now."
HARTLEY: "I love you."
HARTLEY: "So in love."
HARTLEY: "Dude I'm reading our old emails, we're made for
   each other."

We're all free to change our minds about whether we did or did not love a previous paramour, but when you use an institutional apparatus and federal mandates to enforce your change of mind, we've left the realm of the private. Now it's a matter of public concern.

Of course, it's not clear how closely Bobb studied the correspondence. She wrote Ludlow, at one point in the investigation, "I have tried to wade through the various documents that you sent me," and complains that the texts are difficult to read in the format he'd sent because they weren't dated. (He sent her another set, outputted from his phone, with dates.) The word *wade* suggests she found reviewing his side of the case burdensome.

Perhaps this is why the contradictions in Bobb's report are so numerous, though it doesn't explain why the procedural disparities are so glaring. She treated the two entirely unequally, asking Hartley to respond to Ludlow's account; never extending the same opportunity to Ludlow. (Though she did accidentally forward him a message from Hartley effusively thanking Bobb for all her support.) She ignored other evidence Ludlow assembled, including an affidavit about the amicable nature of the relationship from his best friend, Claire, who was so frequently at Ludlow's apartment that Hartley took to referring to her as Ludlow's "husband," which I laughed at—I, too, often found Hartley appealing on paper.

It's just that she seemed to be making a lot of things up. She told Bobb that she felt sorry for Ludlow because she was his only close friend—despite Claire's constant presence. (Claire was also a periodic subject between them in the texts.) She told Bobb that Ludlow was jealous and possessive, which Bobb seemed to believe, despite the numerous texts from Ludlow offering to drive Hartley to and from the airport to visit the Boston boyfriend, along with Hartley's *requests* for rides. When I asked Ludlow why he was driving Hartley to the airport to see another guy, I got the sheepish look. "I don't know," he said.

I suspect it was because he was more in love with Hartley than she was with him and he deferred to her on pretty much everything. It wasn't hard to see why. She was sharp, funny, and feisty. In photos, she has a sexy librarian look, which I understand a lot of men find beguiling. She frequently told him she loved him, and we frequently fall in love with those who seem in love with us too, and sometimes their being a little unavailable isn't an entirely unattractive thing either.

I mentioned earlier that there are often shadowy players and agendas in campus allegations, and Ludlow's case, I'd come to learn, was practically Shakespearean when you started totting up the figures gathered behind the curtains. Though, like Shakespearean servants and gravediggers, they're never content simply to *stay* behind the scenes; they seem compelled to make their presence known. Reading through Bobb's notes, I noticed one such shadowy figure lurking in the margins, and then sprinting into the foreground at odd moments, like a bothersome memory. Let's call him Professor X.

Hartley had told our Title IX officer, Joan Slavin, at their first meeting two years earlier, that Ludlow had a history of dating students. What she didn't say was that she herself had a history of dating professors. In fact, she'd had a previous relationship with another well-known philosophy professor at a previous school. This was Professor X.

Bobb knew about Professor X: Ludlow had brought him up,

and there he is in her notes, with the scrawled comment "not relevant." But to the extent that Bobb's case against Ludlow hinges on the premise (promoted by Hartley, affirmed by Bobb) that Hartley was a spellbound naïf "in awe of Ludlow because he was prominent in the philosophy world and revered in his area of teaching and writing," can Hartley's previous involvement with another influential professor really be entirely irrelevant? After all, if Hartley had been down this road before, she wasn't quite such a naïf.

The ostensible reason Professor X is a recurring figure in the case notes has to do with a research institute in Scotland called Arché. (This may get us a bit into the academic weeds; be forewarned.)

One of Hartley's most damning claims against Ludlow was that during a recruiting weekend for prospective students, he'd offered to arrange a research trip for her there. (He knew the director.) Ludlow had been told to try to recruit Hartley—during a recruiting weekend, you're supposed to recruit promising students, and that's what he was trying to do, he said. Yet now, nearly three years later, Hartley was charging that Ludlow had actually been *grooming* her to be his next conquest by dangling favors. (Note that *grooming* is a term frequently used in conjunction with pedophiles.) Bobb agrees: the Arché offer indicated Ludlow's "attempt to curry favor with Complainant and to begin to foster a dependent relationship with her." Not just dependent, Svengali-like: Hartley was now alleging that Ludlow had "compelled her to come to [Northwestern] and work with him," as though he were some sort of master hypnotist. Bobb (no surprise) confirms it. Thus does graduate recruiting, standard academic practice everywhere, become akin to child sex abuse.

Not knowing much about academic research funds, Bobb also

seems to think Ludlow was offering to foot the bill out of his own pocket. "Don't believe!!" she writes when he "claims" the money for the trip would have come from Northwestern. (Note those multiple exclamation points again.)

Hartley was worried that accepting the funding would look bad, since Ludlow wasn't offering it to other incoming students. So she consulted Professor X about what to do. Interestingly, Professor X took the same position as Ludlow: the idea that Hartley should turn down funding because other students might be jealous was idiotic. Indeed, Professor X actually *called* Jocelyn Packer, Hartley's advisor (in fact, the two were old friends), to weigh in, accusing Packer herself of being sexist for discouraging Hartley from taking the funding. (This is exceedingly odd on many levels, not least the fact that Packer had earlier related the episode to Joan Slavin, for unknown reasons.)

All this is relevant because Arché was crucial for Bobb's case against Ludlow; in fact, she was like a bulldog on the subject. The reason? Precisely because Ludlow never *did* have any evaluative authority over Hartley, so there had to be something else illicit to pin on him. Hence: "grooming." Ludlow was probably even trying to ferry Hartley to another country in order to have his way with her on foreign soil. "Don't believe this was innocent??" Bobb scrawls in her notes. (Ludlow says he'd known Hartley for a half hour at that point and had no sexual interest in her.)

What's rather amazing about all this, though again Bobb seems oblivious, is that the emails Hartley forwarded to Bobb in her efforts to hang Ludlow over the Arché funding had been forwarded to Hartley *from Professor X's account*. His name is in the sender chain. Bobb knew about Hartley's relationship with Professor X, but ignores the implication—which is the uneasy spectacle of one philosophy professor with whom Hartley had had a relationship helping to take down another philosophy professor with whom she'd had a relationship, and *using the secret juridical apparatus of our institution to do it*—a project in which our administration appears to have unwittingly collaborated. (Presumably Hartley forwarded Ludlow's emails to Professor X when they were conferring, and then asked Professor X to forward them back because she'd deleted her copies. Nevertheless.)

Professor X was very much on the scene during Hartley and Ludlow's relationship: the two were still close, and for reasons open to speculation, Hartley lets Ludlow know when they've chatted or he's sent a little gift; his name is scattered throughout their texts. She even had a photo of Professor X on her desk, Ludlow said. Yet Professor X had also acted pretty badly during their relationship, Hartley had told Ludlow—proposing marriage, going so far as to buy her a ring, then getting cold feet and disappearing. (There was a problem: he was already married.)*

Whether Hartley had residual anger or residual sentiment toward Professor X, or how he may have figured in later emotional equations, I don't know. Hartley did text Ludlow, revealingly, the morning after the alleged rape and following Ludlow's attempt to pull the plug on the relationship, "Dude I've been exactly where you are. You're doing exactly what I wished I'd done."

---

* I asked Ludlow if he thought the proposal story was true. He said he'd believed it at the time, but no longer felt he knew what was true and what wasn't.

Ludlow took her to be referring to her situation with Professor X. Of course there was another ongoing triangle: Hartley's Boston boyfriend, about whom she'd expressed a guilty conscience more than once. Given this tangle of men, triangulations, and betrayals, it wouldn't be surprising if identities, culpabilities, and antagonisms occasionally spilled into one another.

A history of dating professors has nothing to do with whether Hartley was or wasn't raped by Ludlow. It does, however, pertain to the portrait of herself she was peddling to Bobb, which Bobb faithfully reproduced: that Hartley had been too "passive, eager to please" with Ludlow, an awestruck innocent swayed by the attentions of a famous professor. I imagine this story would have been harder to uphold if the past relationship with Professor X had been factored in.

So Bobb ignores Professor X. Ludlow has gone down in the history of philosophy as a rapist. Professor X, on the other hand, appears to be professionally thriving. He signs well-meaning petitions protesting sexual misconduct in the discipline.

I asked Ludlow if Professor X had written a recommendation letter for Hartley's admission to Northwestern. He looked surprised and said he hadn't been on the admissions committee, but it was likely, given how close Hartley's philosophical project was to X's work—it would have been considered odd if she *hadn't* had a letter from him. According to Bobb's logic about the Arché funding, even if such a letter predated their relationship, Professor X would have been using it to "groom" Hartley as a future paramour.*

---

* The existence of such a letter would be something of an embarrassment

Bobb couldn't make a finding on the rape, she ultimately concluded, given the friendly texts of the next morning, Hartley's equivocation on the dates, and the fact that she'd told no one else at the time. Yet, based on the Arché business, and other sometimes unintentionally funny conclusions—she treats an unpublished paper Ludlow gave Hartley during recruiting weekend as the equivalent of a billet-doux—even if Ludlow wasn't *technically* Hartley's professor, Bobb decides that a technical reading doesn't go far enough. Why let a technical reading stand in the way of nabbing a predator?

"He took advantage of the unequal power balance between them which arose out of their academic professional relationship as professor/student and mentor/mentee." Also: "In my opinion, she has suffered serious emotional damage as a result of the relationship." Also: "She has no doubt that Ludlow will ruin her in the field."

Evidence? There was none.

It didn't really matter whether or not Bobb found Ludlow guilty of rape, the charge was out there, thus he was guilty of it. Angry feminist philosophers and allies of Hartley continue to recirculate the "rapist" designation on philosophy blogs whenever Ludlow's name comes up, though the disappearance campaign

---

for the philosophy department. Perhaps the reason Professor X kept getting mentioned (not only by Jocelyn Packer—even the philosophy chair brought him up), was bad conscience over knowledge of this previous relationship, which wasn't entirely a secret. Shielding Professor X while hanging Peter Ludlow would be hypocritical at best.

against him has been successful enough that his name comes up less and less frequently.

Ludlow and Hartley had been on decent terms for a while after she ditched him and got back together with her boyfriend, until there was a blowout fight via email, with Hartley furiously reaming Ludlow for, she suspected, revealing their relationship to another senior philosopher. She was angry because she thought her career would be over if word got out; he tells her his career could be at risk, too:

HARTLEY: "You can't lose your job."

LUDLOW: "Watch it happen if you go to the admin."

HARTLEY: "You know I don't have a dishonest bone in my body. I could never do that to anybody."

Not the most self-knowledgeable assessment in the world, it would turn out. Though Hartley was partly right: Ludlow's job wouldn't have been at risk over the relationship—minus the charges of manipulation and nonconsensual sex, that is. (A professor and grad student in my own department recently got married, though they took the precaution of reporting the relationship to the chair when it commenced.)

Speaking of self-knowledge, I must report that the more conversant I became with academic philosophy and its habitués in the course of researching this book, the more I came to think that the historic segmentation of philosophy from psychology (not so divisible for, say, William James, brother of novelist Henry and the philosopher whose *Principles of Psychol-*

ogy launched the field in America) has produced a discipline populated by psychological nincompoops. The self-acuity of the philosophy crowd struck me as an underdeveloped country, though no doubt the same could be said of the sciences, also rife with accusations of sexual misconduct of late. Are the fields that model themselves on the sciences—analytic philosophers, who dominate academic philosophy, lean in this direction, too—more prone to sexual stupidity?* I offer this as a potential research question for further study.

At one point Ludlow himself advanced the theory to me that philosophers choose their subfields based on areas in which they feel lacking—meaning, as he put it, that "someone who's not very eloquent would work in linguistics, someone with an incomplete grasp of facts would work in epistemology." Epistemology, the study of knowledge and knowing, was Hartley's area. I asked Ludlow what someone in the philosophy of language, his own subfield, would be compensating for. "Possibly . . . communicative abilities?" he said, after a considerable pause.

Ludlow was finally able to persuade Hartley he hadn't divulged anything about their relationship to anyone, and things were temporarily better; there was talk about writing a paper together and staying best friends. They bro-hoof, a sign of affection in *My Little Pony* land.

Despite the mutual assurances of lasting devotion, things went bad once again when Ludlow told Hartley, a month after the breakup—perhaps his communicative abilities were indeed

---

* Of course, psychology departments these days, too, tend to be more focused on neural pathways than human depths.

not in top form here—that a philosophy student from another school would be staying in his guest room during a local philosophy conference. This woman had already been a source of tension during their relationship. In conjunction with the conference, there was a party at Ludlow's place. Despite having lambasted him angrily by email just a few days before, Hartley showed up and was, according to Ludlow, both hostile to the visiting student and the last to leave. She gave him a little "so there" flounce at the door on her way out, he recalls. She'd seemed jealous, though he wasn't sure how to interpret that—after all, she'd been the one to break up with him. I asked if he'd been trying to make Hartley jealous by telling her about his houseguest; Ludlow said he'd been trying to *avoid* any scenes—Hartley had been "off the rails" about the woman in the past.

Two weeks later Hartley was summoned to Joan Slavin's office in the Cho investigation. She told Slavin that Ludlow was "a serial sexual predator who targeted vulnerable young women," though Cho's experience with him was unlike her own. (Time line aid: this was two years before Hartley changed her mind and filed charges.)

When I pressed Ludlow on why things had gotten so ugly between the two of them, he mentioned the visiting philosophy student, then speculated that Hartley may have confessed only a small sliver of the infidelity to her then-boyfriend, not the full extent of the relationship. I sensed that, in some perverse way, it was comforting for him to imagine that Hartley's expression of hatred was her way of exorcising her feelings for him, a necessary ritual cleansing performed to consolidate her marriage. When we went over their text exchanges, he pointed out ones he thought indicated that even after the breakup she, too, couldn't completely detach, and read me passages that might support that theory.

Ludlow did help to set up a research trip to Arché for Hartley after their breakup, and this time Hartley took the funding. If one thing's clear, it's that Ludlow had no intention of retaliating against Hartley, as she claimed to fear. "Ludlow will do everything in his power to ruin her career!!" Bobb writes in her notes—more multiple exclamation points—presumably having been assured of it by Hartley. (This would have been well after her return from Arché.) Bobb also cites the post-breakup trip as an example of Ludlow's nefarious use of his institutional power, which seems like having it both ways at once, evidentially speaking.

The irony is that Hartley *should* have taken the funding the first time around. By all accounts, she was a promising student. She and Ludlow were in no way involved at the time. Ludlow's arranging a travel opportunity for a promising student may have been favoritism, but it was deserved favoritism, as both Professor X and Ludlow agreed. It was Hartley's *feminist advisor*, ironically, who told her to turn it down.

The fact is that deserved favoritism, otherwise known as merit, is how things work in our world: Grad students with the most promise get the most opportunities. They get more funding when they enter school, they get more perks along the way, they get invited to conferences, and they get the few remaining good jobs. Grad school is where the winnowing starts, and of course those who get winnowed out are going to protest that the process is biased. How else to account for the fact that others are rising and you're not? Would it have occurred to a guy to wonder why he was being offered funding and the rest of his cohort wasn't? He'd have assumed it was because he was a promising philosopher. Would his advisor have advised him to turn it down? Never. Here you see the convoluted situation of women in academia (though not just academia, of course), especially attractive ones. Obviously they'll be charged with coasting on sex. It had happened to Hartley at her previous school, which had been "riddled with competitive hostility." When she'd once gotten a summer school teaching job, it was "a god damned carnival of innuendo," she wrote Ludlow explaining why she'd decided to decline the first funding offer.

There's a plaintive exchange, following their breakup, with Ludlow asking Hartley why, if she and Professor X had stayed friends, she and Ludlow couldn't do the same. Hartley says that she can't, given her guilt toward her boyfriend (her husband by the time she pressed charges)—with Professor X, *she* hadn't been the one cheating on anyone, so it was different. As this and every other exchange between them makes clear, it wasn't Ludlow calling the shots. His role throughout had been the supplicant, not the seigneur.

The idea that a woman grad student might wield power in a relationship with a male professor was clearly inimical to the cohort of feminist philosophers advising Hartley. This included Hartley's informal advisor, Heidi Lockwood—like Professor X, another of the shadowy figures darting around in the background. (Lockwood was the Southern Connecticut professor who'd advised Hartley to consult a lawyer before meeting with Bobb.) Even minus an official role, Lockwood exerted significant influence on this case: it had been Lockwood, according to Bobb's notes, who convinced Hartley that her consensual relationship with Ludlow *couldn't* have been consensual given the power differential between them.

Watching Lockwood in an online debate about her favorite subject, sexual consent, I detected the wellsprings of Nola Hartley's newfound position about Ludlow, later concretized as "findings" in Patricia Bobb's Title IX report. Did Bobb know she was parroting Lockwood? I doubt it, yet parrot she did.

Lockwood's argument is that sexual *consent* per se isn't the crucial factor in deciding whether sex is consensual; the decisive factor is *context*. Were there unequal power dynamics between the two parties? If yes, how can we say there was consent when the consent may have been coerced, or when subordinated persons don't feel they can say no? For Lockwood, female sexual autonomy itself appears to be more or less a myth: "'Autonomy' presumes . . . that we're not systematically confined by differentials in power or resources or in circumstances and background that can shape those internal processes of judgment."

Her opponent, philosopher Michael Tooley, ventures that *having* power is different from *exercising* power: no one has power over you who doesn't actually attempt to exert that power. The distinction gets no play with Lockwood: there can't be free consent in the context of power asymmetries. One might wish to ask Lockwood how women can ever consent to heterosexual sex in the context of patriarchy if, according to her logic, even pay disparities would wipe out any meaningful consent.

Of course this isn't an original argument on Lockwood's part. It's the position that anti-pornography activists Catharine MacKinnon and Andrea Dworkin took back in the last century, though Lockwood is both expanding their argument and arguably upping its incapacitating effects. She acknowledges that *forcible* sex (the previous era's definition of rape) isn't the problem on campuses these days: the real issue is consent, or the lack of it. Yet she would also shrink any possibility for consent to the point of vanishment. "You can threaten my agency . . . by using the power of your mind to mentally manipulate me, to persuade me," as Lockwood puts it, running down the reasons that sexual autonomy is a myth. So who *can* consent to sex? Not women obviously—how could we? Someone might be mentally manipulating us.

There are indeed multiple asymmetries in relationships, from finances to attractiveness to gender to confidence. And if power differentials make consent impossible, then any person in a position of asymmetrical power (a male, a professor, a high earner) who has sex with a person with less power (a female, a student, a low earner), is effectively a rapist *even if the less-empowered person has consented.*

You begin to see the degree to which consent is a moving target, and the direction in which it's moving on campus is sentimentality about female helplessness. Factor in that sex when either person has been drinking is now typically designated nonconsensual in campus codes—and virtually all sex is fast approaching rape. I don't mean to be hyperbolic, my point is that "rape culture" is less a description of sexual conditions on the ground than an argument about what sex is going to be *designated* consensual and what asymmetries are going to be *designated* significant. Except that we're not actually *having* that argument in any sort of honest or open fashion; instead the bar of consent is being moved around behind closed doors, cloaked in demands for confidentiality and neo-sentimentality about female vulnerability.

Even as the wider culture has moved on, preferring narratives of female agency to the wilting flower thing, on campus it's another story: Lockwood-style views about sex aren't just ascendant in the Dear Colleague era; they've been weaponized in the form of campus codes that paint sex as injurious to women, and rape as the consistent experience. All of which means that even years after the fact, a twenty-five-year-old woman can now change her mind about whether she *really* consented—not just to sex, but to an entire relationship.

Falling into line, Patricia Bobb would ultimately conclude, splitting hairs with the impunity of a papal inquisitor, that Ludlow hadn't *forced* Hartley into a relationship, but—echoing Lockwood—he did *manipulate* her into having one. Of course, to come to this finding requires Bobb to expunge all female intelligence, agency, autonomy, and desire from her calculations. This is supposed to be in women's interests?

Did dating younger women make Ludlow a serial sexual predator, as Nola Hartley assured Joan Slavin? It's true that he'd had a three-year relationship with a former student, though that's only the same as being a predator if women are children, or otherwise incapable of sexual consent. Look, if I got to impose my vision of sexual morality on the world, everyone would find age-appropriate mates; also human sexual intelligence would be such that everyone would avoid workplace entanglements, which, as any sentient human knows, often end badly. But I can't say that in my own case I've consistently met these standards, so who am I to issue prescriptions?

Of course, Ludlow wasn't the only one with relationship patterns; perhaps Hartley veered toward a certain type too, as previously discussed. But speaking of seriality, it falls to me to mention that Hartley was also a serial Title IX complainant. At the time she initiated the complaint against Ludlow, she'd filed only one previous Title IX complaint, against a fellow grad student (and one-time friend) she charged with sexual harassment over an incident that took place even before she'd enrolled at Northwestern. He'd importuned his way into her hotel room during a philosophy conference in Evanston, she said, showing up at her door drunk and crying, refusing to leave. He cried so much she had to let him in, she'd later told Ludlow, and he spent the night in her room. At a second conference, a few months later, as recorded in Bobb's notes, the grad student and Hartley were once again flirting, though he knew he was competing with Professor X for Hartley's attentions; unfortunately Professor X won. (Indeed the two were spotted kissing—Professor X minus his wedding ring, I was told.)

The hotel room story, reported by Hartley to Joan Slavin, wasn't so unlike the one Hartley later told Bobb about being compelled to stay at Ludlow's place to assuage his loneliness. "He was needy and wanted her to spend all her time with him," as Bobb recapped Hartley's plaint. Male pathos keeps forcing Hartley into situations not of her choosing—as it does all of us tenderhearted women, I suppose. The grad student was put on probation for a quarter (and would later have trouble getting funding from the department as a result, Ludlow said).

Hartley seems like one of those people who leave a lot of drama in her wake. Bobb knew about this previous Title IX charge, as did Ludlow—in fact, Ludlow says Bobb asked him if it had worried him about Hartley. Maybe it should have. To date, she's filed *six* Title IX complaints—or six that I know of. The four to come

I'll take up in the next chapter. Two of them were against me, which probably colors my thinking about serial charge-bringers. (Yes, Hartley would go on to be my accuser too, after she was Ludlow's.)

Hartley did complain more than once about sexual harassment, Ludlow mentioned, when I asked him why she hadn't just sent the importuning grad student packing instead of letting him into her hotel room. He recalled one complaint about a visiting professor making a toast to "new friends," which Hartley took to be about her. Yet rather than raising questions about her propensity to find injury, her complaints made Ludlow feel special—like she was confirming that *he* wasn't "one of the dirtbags," he said, with not a little self-irony.

Serial charge-bringing is a dangerous proclivity for others in the immediate vicinity. Based on Hartley's Title IX complaints and Bobb's findings, the university instituted dismissal proceedings against Ludlow, even though the relationship hadn't been against any code, even though Bobb hadn't found against Ludlow on the nonconsensual sex allegation, and even though Hartley had a history as a complaint filer.

"I can promise you that you will always have me in your life," Hartley had texted Ludlow, the morning after the night she'd later say he raped her. "And that I'll always love you. So much."

I can't say that I entirely understand Hartley, though I've certainly spent a lot of time pondering her. At one point Ludlow said to me, when I laughed at one of the text exchanges between the two of them—Hartley's funny snarkiness was in full form— "You would have liked her back then."

The change from then to now was startling though. In the 2011 texts, Hartley is confident, funny, and in control. She puts Ludlow in his place, she argues philosophy, she upbraids him when she's peeved. There's not an iota of intimidation or deference. In one exchange early on in the relationship, she proposes that the two of them get together, and Ludlow responds with a smiley emoticon. Hartley texts back, "We need to have a talk about how I feel about emoticons . . ." and then, rather instructively, "'Use your words.'" It's what parents say to their kids. This is someone in command of herself and the situation.

By March 2014, in her statements to Bobb, she'd come to view herself through a scrim of bathos. "I'm a shadow of my former self," she tells Bobb. I truly didn't understand how someone who'd once had a lot of spunk and originality could have spoken such a canned sentence unless she were playing a role. (Maybe she was: she repeated the very same phrase to a reporter from the *Chronicle* a year later—she also said she'd never considered her relationship with Ludlow romantic, nor had they dated.) Having been taken up by a trio of feminist advisors hadn't done her much good—to the contrary, it seems to have transformed her into either a not very bright child, or a chronic dissembler.

Freud remarks somewhere that to achieve a "passive aim" may call for a large amount of activity. It was a line that often crossed my mind when thinking about this saga, and the style of passive-aggressive femininity that's become ascendant, and institutionally endorsed, on our campuses.

One of the limitations of treating male sexuality as a primordial danger is that what's dangerous is also alluring. Of course, as everyone knows, attraction can also flip into repulsion in an instant. Demanding institutional solutions to these essential human dichotomies is turning us into a society of sexual liars. The tough question becomes how colleges and universities can deal adequately with the external realities of sexual assault on the one hand and the inner realities of sexual ambivalence on the other, without building an accusation machinery so vast and indiscriminate that it becomes a magnet for neurotic schemes, emotional knife play, and monstrously self-exonerating agendas.

3

My Title IX Inquisition

THE "SAFER" THE SPACE, THE MORE
DANGEROUS FOR PROFESSORS

The email to me from Joan Slavin was uninformative in the extreme. The subject heading was "Title IX Complaints": "I am writing to inform you that two students have filed Title IX retaliation complaints against you with the University on the basis of statements made in your recent *Chronicle* article and subsequent public statements."

The essay had been out for a couple of weeks at that point and was causing a bit of a ruckus. I'd been so swamped with emails I could barely glance at them, but the opening line of this one gave me a jolt. I read on. The university was retaining an outside law firm to conduct an investigation of me; the investigators would be in touch. A link was provided where I might learn more about Title IX and the university's policies, though when I clicked on it, it just led to more links. I couldn't find anything explaining how you could get brought up on Title IX complaints for writing an essay.

A lot of people wondered the same thing. A year or so later, a bunch of law professors wrote in an "Open Letter Regarding Campus Free Speech and Sexual Assault" that the OCR's 2014 Resolution Agreement with Harvard Law School, which mandated that Harvard was obligated to consider the effect of off-campus conduct, was considered to be the legal basis for "a subsequent probe by Northwestern of a faculty member who had published an article" (this was me). No one ever said anything quite so explanatory to me at the time.

"Please be advised that retaliation against people for filing complaints and participating in the investigation process is prohibited," Slavin's email concluded. "Finally, as with all complaints, I ask that as a respondent to these complaints, you keep this matter confidential. Thank you."

Clicking on the links produced by the first Title IX link brought me to pages containing more links and more policies. It was hyperlink hell. Additional clicking produced information on the rights of accusers and what to do if you'd been harassed, but nothing that related to me. I did learn that Title IX protects individuals who've reported sexual misconduct from retaliation (characterized as "intimidation, threats, coercion, or discrimination"), but I failed to see how I could have retaliated against anyone when it wasn't me who'd been charged with sexual misconduct in the first place. The *Chronicle* essay had also named no one by name. In fact, I didn't actually know the names of Ludlow's accusers at the time.

My first encounter with the student I've been calling Nola Hartley had been in the pages of one of the lawsuits Peter Ludlow filed, which I'd perused while writing the *Chronicle* essay, though her name was redacted. She was identified only as "PHD STUDENT." In the wording of the lawsuit, "Defendant PHD STUDENT was a graduate student at the time," which, because of the past tense and an overly literal tendency, I mistakenly took to mean a former grad student rather than a current one. Hartley would later charge (illogically, I felt) that I could have found out her name if I'd tried, but why would I have tried?

In that Hartley would become an antagonist, it was ironic that my initial instinct was actually to protect her. There was a fair amount of personal and sexual information about the unnamed grad student in the pages of the lawsuit, including that she'd had a previous relationship with a previous professor (Professor X). There were details about the nonconsensual sex allegation against Ludlow, that they'd continued to have sex after the alleged episode, and that the charge hadn't been upheld by the Title IX investigator. It sounded like a relationship gone wrong, as distinct from the situation with Cho, and it didn't seem necessary to recirculate any of this. I confined myself to a few short paragraphs about Cho's case, which sufficiently exemplified the tenor of campus sexual paranoia I meant to indict. Cho had by then filed lawsuits against both the university and Ludlow, occasioning a flurry of back-and-forth actions and filings among the parties, which had become an ongoing legal morass, meaning all this was already in the public record.

The *Chronicle* essay was over five thousand words. *Seven* of these words were about Hartley—she was a clause in a list of people Ludlow was suing for defamation. The seven words were "a former grad student he previously dated."

Soon after the essay came out a flurry of objections arrived at the *Chronicle's* editorial offices, sent by various Hartley allies insisting that Ludlow and Hartley *hadn't* "dated"—this was merely Ludlow's version of events. I'd gotten emails to this effect, too, which I'd glanced at but hadn't really read (to be honest, I don't read angry emails about what I write, in case you're planning on sending one). From what I could tell they were objecting to my point of view, which I wasn't going to change, and in any case the essay was already in print.

I didn't believe Ludlow and the grad student hadn't dated—there was sufficient detail in the pages of his lawsuit to convince me they had. Still, over my mild objections, the *Chronicle* amended the online version to read "a former grad student whom, according to his complaint, he had previously dated." Now there were thirteen words about Hartley, almost double from where we'd started. I'm not sure why they never removed that "former," which actually was incorrect. I regret the error.

But the outraged letters kept arriving, including a rambling letter from Hartley herself, pasted inside an email sent by someone else. I glanced at the first few lines. She seemed to be complaining that I should have written about how damaged she'd been by Peter Ludlow. It seemed to me her point of view had been sufficiently represented; in fact, it had prevailed as the official story. There was a letter from Hartley's advisor Jocelyn Packer, which I also didn't read, though I did reply, "Thank you for writing"—she was, after all, a colleague and I was trying to be collegial.

Packer would later write to the *Chronicle*'s editors informing them that I'd been brought up on Title IX complaints, and advising them to distance themselves from me. It was like being tattled on to the teacher. I did find it outrageous that Title IX was being wielded as a club to discredit someone (*me*) with an employer—was she trying to get me blacklisted too, along with Ludlow?

If word gets around that Title IX can be used by one professor to try to shut down a rival professor's point of view, I foresee potential complainants lining up around the block.

All this made me wonder whether Packer had advised her students to file the Title IX complaints against me—she did seem rather invested in the situation. If so, it was spectacularly dumb advice. I knew from the moment I opened the email from Joan Slavin that this was going to be a shit storm. I didn't know how it was going to play out, but I was pretty sure neither the complainants nor the university was going to come out looking good, even though, at that point, I still had no idea who the complainants were.

I also knew next to nothing about Title IX, but we were still living in America (or so I thought), and either the place had turned into a police state without my noticing, or using a federal law against gender discrimination to punish a professor for writing an essay was something other people were likely to find outrageous too.

So there I was, staring at Slavin's confusing email. I wrote back asking for clarification: when would I learn the specifics of these complaints, which, I pointed out, appeared to violate my academic freedom? And what about *my* rights—was I entitled to a lawyer? I received a polite response from Slavin with a link to another website. No, I could not have an attorney present during the investigation, unless I'd been charged with sexual violence. (Of course Ludlow *had* been charged with sexual violence yet was told he couldn't have an attorney, I'd later learn—consistency isn't a big element in Title IX adjudications.) I could have a "support person" from the university community, though that person would be prohibited from speaking. Also, I wouldn't be informed about the substance of the complaints until I met with the investigators.

Apparently the idea was that they'd tell me the charges, and then, while I was collecting my wits, interrogate me about them. The term *kangaroo court* came to mind. I wrote back to ask for the charges in writing. Slavin wrote back thanking me for my "thoughtful questions."

What I very much wanted to know, though there was apparently no way of finding it out, was whether this was the first instance of Title IX charges filed over a publication. Was this a test case? It seemed to pit a federally mandated program against my constitutional rights, though I admit my understanding of those rights was vague.

A week or so later, I heard from the investigators. For reasons I didn't understand at the time, Northwestern, which is just north of Chicago, had hired an outside law firm based in Kansas City, a ninety-minute flight away, to investigate me. A team of two lawyers had been appointed, and they wanted to schedule "an initial interview" the following week. The word *initial* worried me— how many "interviews" were they planning? They were available to fly in to meet in person—the words *billable hours* came to mind—or we could video-conference. Their email contained *even more* links to more Title IX websites, each of which contained still more links. I had the feeling that clicking on any of them would propel me into an informational black hole where I'd learn nothing, yet not reemerge for days.

I'd spoken to a lawyer on the phone by then, who gave me useful tips on how to respond to these requests. (A practical aside: I advise anyone, professor or student, summoned to a Title IX meeting to contact a lawyer *immediately*. Ignore the fucking links: your rights are the last thing on anyone's mind.) I wrote back that I wanted to know the charges before agreeing to a meeting. My investigators responded, cordially, that they wanted to set up a meeting during which they would inform me of the charges and pose questions. I replied, in what I hoped was a cordial tone, that I wouldn't answer questions until I'd had time to consider the charges.

We finally agreed to schedule a Skype session in which they would inform me of the charges and I would *not* answer questions. I felt the flush of victory, though it was short-lived. I said I wanted to record the session; they refused but said I could take notes. The reasons for these various interdictions were never explained, which is par for the course in every Title IX investigation I've since heard about. You have no idea what your rights are; you have no idea what the procedures are; you have no idea if what you might say will later be used to hang you.

I'd been plunged into an underground world of secret tribunals and capricious, medieval rules, and I wasn't supposed to tell anyone about it.

One of the more informative documents that came my way later, after I'd broken all the rules and gone public about my case, was the transcript of a Listserv conversation among a handful of Title IX professionals discussing exactly the procedural questions that had baffled me throughout the investigation. Here was an amazing chance to eavesdrop on what the inquisitors say when they think no one's listening.

The discussion was about the optimal moment to tell "respondents," professors or students, the specifics of the charges filed against them. How long should investigators withhold this information for strategic purposes? It turns out there's no established or nationally uniform set of procedures; each institution devises its own. Naturally this leaves a lot of leeway, especially for those who enjoy power a little too much. (I suspect this isn't without a gendered dimension: there's no doubt in my mind that female Title IX officers handed a rare opportunity to put male sexuality on trial are responsible for quite a bit of Title IX overreach. It's payback time, gentlemen.)

The split in this particular crowd was between strategic types who favored not revealing too much to respondents and those who questioned the ethics of withholding information—or, as I came to think of them, Title IX hawks versus Title IX doves, of which there appeared to be only one.

The hawks styled themselves as pragmatists, not hawks: they felt that revealing too much to a respondent risked sullying the integrity of the findings. "I firmly believe that part of the job of a well-trained, professional investigator is to minimize the possibility that any witness will lie to them," said A, who advised parceling information out slowly, watching how the charged person responded, and then applying amateur psychology to assess innocence or guilt.

B agreed. "I want to watch their reactions to hearing the allegations for the first time. That is really important to me, and I also believe it cuts down on fabrication."

A clarified, "For me it's not so much the visible reaction I am looking for but their initial version of what happened, which may be more accurate. An innocent person has nothing to hide and should not be worried about sharing the truth. If a person has done something wrong, he or she is likely to look for ways to cover that up."

(This sounded familiar. Oh, right—it's what the FBI, CIA, and NSA are always saying: you don't need civil rights if you haven't done anything wrong.)

C (the dove) objected: "You have no idea what's going on in a person's head, and reading the expressions of a person being told something the first time is not necessarily reliable, unless you are an expert in micro-expressions. Most of the signs people use as indicators of credibility are false. The vast majority of people are going to be angry, upset, etc [when hearing charges against them]. How do you know whether face-flushing, crying, or anger means I'm responsible for something, or it just means I'm embarrassed or angry?"

A argued, "My role is not to enable a responsible party to defend their innocence; my role is to be impartial and to seek the truth." First he asks for the respondent's account of what happened. Only then does the respondent get a copy of the complaint information. "I give the respondent a period of time to reflect on the written complaint and provide me with his or her written response. I look for consistency between the respondent's initial account and his or her written response, because inconsistencies can possibly relate to credibility."

C: "These are educational institutions, not police precincts. I don't think we need to treat people like criminals to begin with. What I'm looking for is a humane process that gives people the opportunity to respond without feeling threatened, to the best of our ability."

Someone else asked, "Have you ever had anyone turn around and say, gee, I'm going to have to go think about this?"

"Yes," B responded. "They listen to the allegations and refuse to make a statement. Not entirely uncommon."

Nevertheless, to C, withholding info was unfair: "Can you imagine showing up to a trial and not knowing the specifics?"

There was more, but let this suffice. Having been on the other side of the process, reading this conversation left me seething—also because I've now heard from so many panicked students and professors who were summoned to mysterious meetings and then sandbagged, whose futures and jobs were on the line, who were confronted with rumors and false information by condescending and mysteriously empowered functionaries who seemed to be making up the rules as they went along. As it turns out, they were.

Since I strongly believe that the Title IX process should be far more transparent than it is, let me introduce some transparency by telling you everything I can remember about everything that happened to me during mine. I hope this will prove useful should you find yourself up on Title IX complaints someday too.

I'll begin with the Skype session with the investigators, where I first learned who my complainants were. (I was very relieved to learn that neither was one of *my* students). I didn't know either of them. In fact, one had nothing whatsoever to do with the essay. She was bringing charges on behalf of "the university community" as well as on behalf of Eunice Cho and Nola Hartley, even though Hartley was herself the second complainant. (I never learned whether Eunice Cho was actually consulted about the complaints brought in her name.)

Let's pause to note that "third-party complaints" are permissible under Title IX. Here's a working definition of "third-party complaint." At the moment a legal case is pending against the Office for Civil Rights itself, by a male student charged with having nonconsensual sex with a consenting woman. The woman has said repeatedly that the sex was consensual. The problem came when a friend of hers spotted a hickey on her neck and reported it. The accused student, who was black, by the way, and attending school on an athletic scholarship, received a multi-year suspension, effectively ending his college career. That's what "third-party complaint" means.

My first complainant was charging that my essay had had a "chilling effect" on students' ability to report sexual misconduct, and that I'd made deliberate mistakes. Referring to Hartley as a former rather than current graduate student was one. The other was that I'd mistaken the number of lawsuits Cho had filed that had been turned down—I'd said "several." I think one suit had been turned down at that point, and another hadn't been allowed to proceed. (There had been a flurry of motions, suits, and counter-suits, and I'd lost track.) Also the essay violated the non-retaliation provision of our university's faculty handbook, she charged, though her notion of "retaliation" seemed extremely elastic.

The second complainant, Hartley, charged that merely mentioning her in the essay was retaliatory and created a hostile environment, though I'd said nothing disparaging in those seven words, "a former grad student he previously dated." Also, I'd omitted information I *should* have included about her, she said. Again, this seemed paradoxical: is what I *didn't* write the business of Title IX? She further charged that something I'd tweeted to someone else regarding the essay had actually referred to her.

Please pause to note that a Title IX charge can now be brought

137

against a professor over a tweet. Also note that my tweets were being monitored. The tweet in question—a response to someone I didn't know named @lemonhound, who'd tweeted something to me regarding my essay, and the catastrophic effects of students dating professors—was: "It's a problem that 'trauma' is now deployed re any bad experience. And dating is not the same as rape!" The tweet wasn't about Hartley.

Apparently she wished it had been. At some level, Hartley's relation to me seemed as convoluted as her relation to Ludlow. She wanted something from me (to tell her story, to be on her side), even though she didn't want to be written about, while also wanting to punish me for not having done so extensively enough. Believe me, I sympathize with convoluted desires; I have plenty of them myself. And I understand the tortuous relation of graduate students to professors, simultaneously hating and desiring us for having lives and careers they aspire to and fear they'll never attain, especially in today's job market, which makes every issue connected to status and hierarchy feel all the more wounding. It still doesn't mean that Title IX offices should provide the settings to act out psychodramas better dealt with through introspection or therapy.

Since the investigators refused to provide the charges in writing and I can often barely read my own handwriting, I typed notes during our Skype session, feeling like an incompetent secretary. I wondered if they'd object to that, too—could they? The extent of their powers was mysterious to me. I'd briefly considered furtively recording the session despite the ban, but decided against it—I'm a law-abiding type, I discovered to my chagrin.

Why would they refuse to give me the charges in writing? Perhaps so they could watch my face as I heard them, via the forensic magic of Skype.

Later I made what sense I could of my wildly mistyped notes and emailed the investigators a summary, adding that I'd answer only questions related to the charges I'd been informed about, as advised in my phone consultation with the lawyer. (They didn't respond.) Then I wrote up a peevish statement asserting that my essay had been political speech, stemming from my belief, *as a feminist*, that women have spent the past century and a half demanding to be treated as consenting adults and now a cohort on campuses was demanding we relinquish those rights, which was a disastrous move for feminism. I used the words *political* and *feminist* numerous times. (They didn't respond to that either.)

What I really wanted to know from them was this: Who decided that intellectual disagreement can be *officially* construed as retaliation, and that a professor can be charged for writing about a legal case that's been nationally reported precisely because she's employed by the university where the events took place? Wouldn't this mean that academic freedom doesn't extend to academics discussing matters involving their own workplaces?

Let me add that I don't think my university necessarily wanted to be the venue for a free-speech face-off. Indeed, our president had himself recently published an op-ed in the *Wall Street Journal* in defense of academic freedom. I never really learned if any Title IX charge that's filed has to go forward (this was later a matter of dispute), though in the aftermath, the university took the public position that their only choice had been to launch the investigation machinery.

The fact is, and as my case revealed, *no one* knows what Title

IX demands of universities. University presidents don't know, Title IX officers themselves don't know. Title IX officers I've spoken to say (not for attribution) that the Dear Colleague letters are incoherent and that everyone's left trying to figure out how to comply with insufficient and wildly contradictory directives. This means, in effect, that anyone on campus is empowered to decide on and radically expand the Title IX purview, including designating ideological opponents as creators of hostile environments.[*]

The reality is that the more that colleges devote themselves to creating "safe spaces," that new campus watchword, the more dangerous campuses have become for professors, and the less education itself becomes anyone's priority. A lot has been written about this in the last couple of years (including in response to my own case), so I'll keep it brief. Let me just say that nearly every academic I know—this includes feminists, progressives, minorities, and those who identify as gay or queer—now lives in fear of some classroom incident spiraling into professional disaster. After the sexual paranoia essay ran, I was deluged with emails from professors applauding what I'd written because they were

---

[*] In my newfound role as poster person for Title IX overreach, I was invited to speak to a convention of Title IX officers held in Philadelphia in October 2016, a prospect that made me profoundly nervous, though I found the attendees surprisingly congenial. Among the many interesting things I learned was that a significant percentage of them actively hate the OCR. The group sponsoring the convention—ATIXA (Association of Title IX Administrators), headed by attorney Brett Sokolow—appears to be trying to rein in the extremes of Title IX vigilantism, recognizing that such excesses invite scrutiny and unwelcome pushback by the courts and, potentially, Congress.

too frightened to say such things publicly themselves. My in-box was bursting with reports about student accusations and sensitivities, and the collective terror of sparking them.

Among other things, I learned that professors, even at major research universities, now routinely avoid discussing subjects in class that might raise hackles. A well-known sociologist wrote that he no longer lectures on abortion. I spoke to an Ivy League law professor whose students won't attend lectures about rape law. Someone who'd written a book about incest in her own family described being confronted in class by a student furious with her for discussing the book. A tenured female professor on my campus wrote about lying awake at night worrying that some stray remark of hers might lead to student complaints, social media campaigns, eventual job loss, and her being unable to support her child. I'd thought at the time that she was exaggerating, but that was before I learned I myself was a Title IX respondent.

My midwestern Torquemadas were perfectly pleasant at our on-campus meeting—they'd indeed flown to town to meet me in person. They were both youngish (thirties, I'd guess), dressed in the sort of business wear you don't see much on campus. Indeed, they were so pleasant that I relaxed and became overvoluble, stupidly gratified by their interest and attentions. There I was, expounding on my views about power and feminism; soon I was delivering a mini-seminar on the work of Michel Foucault. Later, replaying the three-hour session in my mind, I thought, "You chump," realizing that I'd probably dug a hundred new holes for myself.

They asked endless questions about the sources for my ideas

and claims, about particular sentences in the essay, and what I'd meant in that fateful tweet. There were fishing expedition questions—the lawyer had warned me not to answer these—such as what I'd do if a student reported a sexual harassment incident to me. They asked if I'd been in contact with Ludlow; I said I'd once written him (long before I was commissioned by the *Chronicle*) to ask if I could interview him; he'd replied that he wasn't able to do interviews. I had the impression they already knew this—I later reflected that I'd written him on my university account and wondered if they'd dipped into my emails.

Or was this paranoia? Everything that's said about being the subject of an investigation is true—it evokes some sort of primal guilt (the inner territory Kafka claimed as his métier), and even if you think you're in the right, your defenses start sounding a little thin, even to yourself.[*]

Some of their questions were intrusive and irrelevant. A few times I said "I'm not going to answer that," at which point the pleasantness dropped, and the prosecutor emerged. "You opened the door to it," said my interrogator as I tried, feeling stupid, to reconstruct the last few sentences in my by-then enfogged brain.

They didn't record any of this, nor was there a stenographer. One of the lawyers typed notes on her laptop; they'd send me a summary of my remarks, they said, which I could correct or add to, if I chose. I found these procedures utterly mystifying. Why no transcript?

---

[*] Actually it wasn't paranoia—I later spoke to a faculty member who'd shown up for a meeting with university lawyers and been presented with printouts from her email account.

In light of the many horror stories I've heard about despotic treatment in Title IX cases, I have to say I was treated extremely courteously. Toward the end, I asked, with a certain irritation, how the complainants could possibly know that my essay had created a "chilling effect" on campus, which seemed unverifiable at best. "It's a pretty big campus," I pointed out. One complainant, I was told, had provided the lawyers with the names of students and staff members (I believe seven) who would testify that my essay had chilled them. I, too, could supply names of witnesses to interview, they offered cheerfully. I declined.

As I was leaving, one of the lawyers stopped me at the door. "You know the students are worried you're going to write about this too."

"Oh, I *absolutely* plan to write about it," I said.

At that point I was sick of them both, pleasant or not, and tired from three hours of answering their questions. Also, despite my best attempts to stay cool about things, in the weeks leading up to the meeting, I was routinely waking up at four in the morning with the questions I assumed they'd be asking replaying in my mind. I was angry about all the disrupted sleep—I'm one of those people who can't function if I don't sleep. And even though I was fairly confident I wasn't going to be fired, the fact that the higher-ups were willing to go as far as they did surprised the shit out of me. It didn't seem unlikely that I'd be censured in some way, forced to go to sensitivity training or some other humiliation, if only to throw a bone to the complainants, and this made me angry in advance, partly because I knew enough about them by this point to know they'd crow about it publicly.

The reason I suspected so was this: shortly before our meeting, one of the complainants published an online article on a well-trafficked site excoriating my sexual paranoia essay and announcing that two unnamed students had filed Title IX retaliation complaints against me. It was obvious the article's author was one of the complainants: she revealed no other sources for the confidential info she was exposing, and it was clear she was well versed on all the inside details. The irony was that it made any expectation of confidentiality from me moot, or that was my view. (Had she really not considered that?)

But it wasn't me alone on the chopping block: the article also excoriated our university president for his *Wall Street Journal* essay on academic freedom, which, the author charged, had been a veiled commentary on the Title IX case against me and thus subverted the Title IX process by issuing a covert advance verdict in my favor. (The president had obliquely mentioned the protest march against the essay, among other campus free-speech issues, but nothing about Title IX.) Yet wasn't she herself subverting the process by publicly charging that the process had been subverted, not to mention by revealing the complaints against me?

If a grad student can publicly blast her own university's president, mock his ideas, and fear no repercussions, then clearly the retaliatory power that university employment confers on anyone, from professors to presidents, is nil. Nor had my own essay exactly had a chilling effect on anyone's freedom of expression, to say the least. The article neatly demolished its own premises about the asymmetries of institutional power by the very fact of its publication.

At the close of the meeting with the investigators, they asked if I wanted to file my own retaliation complaint against the complainant for revealing the charges against me. I declined to press charges against anyone.

That was my only face-to-face meeting with the investigators, though there were numerous phone calls, emails, and requests for further substantiation. I gave them copies of emails with my *Chronicle* editor about fact-checking, and copies of tweets, and copies of the redacted lawsuits I'd drawn on. I tried to guess what all this was costing—two lawyers flying back and forth to conduct interviews with the complainants, me, and an expanding list of witnesses; reviewing the sources for a 5,200-word article; adjudicating their findings; and composing a thorough report. I'm no expert on legal fees, but I was pretty sure the meter was ticking up in $10,000 increments. I later learned that a similar investigation on another campus had cost over $148,000—this was the University of Colorado–Boulder philosopher, David Barnett, whose case I'll be getting to. I felt competitive about it, and hoped mine had cost more. After all, I had *two* lawyers from out of state; Barnett's guy was just hopping in his car and driving over from Denver.

I'd been told there would be a report within sixty days—this is mandated by Title IX—though on what basis they'd make their findings, I had no idea. The standard that applied was preponderance of evidence, of course, though note that I was never actually *presented* with any of this evidence. Given that the investigators doubled as judge and jury, I wished I'd been more ingratiating.

I heard nothing. A month went by. I tried to ignore the whole thing, though it felt like something hanging over me. I half-hoped I'd be found guilty, which I fantasized would create a constitutional collision between Title IX and some other branch of government that would step in to stand up for free speech.* I started drafting a new essay about my experiences as a Title IX offender.

When I finally got a call from the investigators at the sixty-day mark, it wasn't about the resolution; it was to let me that *new* Title IX complaints had been filed *against my faculty support person.* I'd asked the president of the Faculty Senate to accompany me to the meeting. I knew him slightly—we'd socialized a few times years before, and he seemed like a reliable ally, but he was so outraged about the case that he couldn't contain himself. He issued objections throughout the interrogation, which was supposedly verboten. Then, believing the process he'd witnessed was a violation of academic freedom, and as a member of the Faculty Senate, whose bylaws include the protection of academic freedom, he decided to speak out at a senate meeting about my case.

My complainants got word, of course—Jocelyn Packer's husband was a faculty senator—and were incensed at my support person for breaking confidentiality about the case. Hence the new Title IX complaints. This despite the fact that the Title IX case against me had already been revealed by the complainant's article, and by Professor Packer to the *Chronicle* editors. Were these people mad?

So now my support person could no longer act as my support

---

* The House Judiciary Committee did hold hearings on First Amendment protections at *public* colleges and university campuses in June 2015, and my case did come up—with no discernable effect on the Title IX juggernaut.

person, the investigators told me curtly, as though *I'd* had something to do with it. Another team of lawyers from the same firm was being appointed to conduct a new investigation, they said. This firm was really cleaning up, I thought.

A few days later I learned, via back channels, that my indefatigable complainants had also filed Title IX complaints against *the president of the university* over his *Wall Street Journal* op-ed. What was there to do but laugh—the whole thing was a circus, and the university just kept hiring new teams of lawyers to sweep up the tent. Of course I understood why: they couldn't be seen as *lax* on Title IX compliance.

Seventy-two days after the investigation commenced, the *Chronicle* ran the piece I'd written about the process, "My Title IX Inquisition," even though I was still waiting to hear the outcome of the case. There was an immediate commotion on social media, and in the real media, too. No one had thought that in America you could get put on trial for writing an essay, especially a secret trial where they refused to put the charges against you in writing.

Around 6:00 p.m. the same day, twelve hours after the piece went online, I got an email from the lead investigator telling me that I had been cleared of all the charges. There were two five-page summaries of their findings attached, one for each case.

A few days later, I got another email, from a *second* team of lawyers from the same firm, telling me that the complaints against my faculty support person had been withdrawn. They included another piece of information no one had mentioned previously, which was that *more* Title IX complaints had been filed against me, by the same complainants, along with the complaints against my support person. This second team of lawyers had been secretly investigating those new complaints, concerning *my* "potential involvement in and/or approval of [my support person's] recent comments during a meeting of the Northwestern University Faculty Senate." They'd been preparing to notify me, they wrote.

These additional complaints against me had also been withdrawn, I now learned. Shortly later, I heard that the complaints against the president had been withdrawn at the same time. Presumably there had been a third team of lawyers hired to investigate him.

As far as I knew, there were now no outstanding complaints against me, though there was a twelve-day window during which the complainants could file an appeal if they chose. Given their doggedness, I figured I shouldn't yet assume I was in the clear, but the complainants themselves announced the verdict online, disputing that they'd ever tried to infringe on my academic freedom. The only issue was factual errors in my piece, they asserted, falsely, in various anonymous online posts.

A week or so before I received the resolution letters saying I was cleared, the investigators had phoned to let me know that a "mediated resolution" was possible in my case if I wished to pursue that option. I asked what that meant—an image of myself and the complainants in a conference room hugging came to mind; I didn't like the visual. The students were willing to drop their complaints in exchange for a public apology from me, the investigators said. I tried to stifle a laugh. I asked if that was all. No, they also wanted me to agree not to write about the case. At this point a snort escaped. One of the lawyers said good-naturedly, "We thought you'd respond that way; we just had to ask."

Who knows you better than your inquisitors?

There was a curious passage in the resolution letters I received. Because of the "unique nature" of the cases, I'd have a two-week window to review a redacted version of the two full reports. I couldn't take notes or make photocopies, but I could sit in a room with a paralegal present and read them. This offer came as a surprise: it's a private institution and bound by no requirements to let anyone see anything. Yet here they were, giving the fox the keys to the chicken coop, though a fox with a terrible memory, admittedly—if I couldn't take notes, I didn't know how much practical use reading the reports was going to be.

What prompted the informational largesse? Was it for my benefit, or the complainants'? Universities aren't monolithic places, and it occurred to me that a few higher-ups might not be entirely opposed to a contrarian feminist professor taking on the excesses of Title IX in some future venue, but that's just speculation.

At the appointed hour, I showed up and was steered to an anonymous conference room. I carefully placed my handbag and its stash of contraband pens in a corner out of arm's reach (I had a cold and asked for permission to place my tissues nearby), then read through two separate *sixty-page single-spaced reports*. Only at this point did I finally learn what the actual complaints against me had been, though some of it I'd inferred from the nature of the questions I'd been asked.

I also learned that the investigators had been thorough beyond belief—I could see why preparing these reports had taken them seventy-two days. A lot of it was boring: detailed enumeration of codes and hairsplitting about their applicability to the current situation, which I won't go into because I don't remember the specifics. But there were two things that surprised me immensely.

The first was that the investigators had bent over backward to clear me.

Just one example: Among Hartley's complaints was my use of the word *dated* to describe her relationship with Ludlow. I'd settled on this word because it was the most innocuous one I could think of to describe what I knew about their relationship at that point, which had involved dating-like activities such as dining, traveling, and sleeping in the same bed. I'd debated whether to say "relationship" or "involved with," and settled on "dated" because it didn't purport to gauge the emotional tenor of whatever had transpired.

Of course, Hartley was now calling what had taken place between her and Ludlow "a deeply inappropriate relationship." There had been some testy back-and-forth between me and the investigators on this point, with one of them finally exclaiming, "You *know* she says he raped her." I said my understanding was that the rape charge hadn't been upheld. I got the distinct impression that they assumed Ludlow was guilty of rape, despite there being no finding on it in Bobb's investigation.

So I was amazed to discover they'd consulted a half dozen different dictionaries and listed maybe ten different definitions of the word *date*, to demonstrate that there were so many possible meanings that I couldn't be held to one of them. Even two people eating together in a restaurant, regardless of romantic or sexual interest, was sufficient to qualify as dating, they wrote.

In none of the Title IX cases I've learned about in the last year did investigators do research to clear a respondent. It's invariably the reverse, as in Ludlow's case—exculpating evidence is ignored. Having now read or heard about so many slipshod and illogical Title IX reports, the thoroughness in my case astounds me all the more. Obviously I was pleased to be found in the right, but I'm still curious about the motives.

Were they more inclined to work so vigorously to clear me because they knew I planned to write about the investigation? Or was it because they, too, thought the charges were bogus? Either way, it seems clear that the case had to come out in my favor. If I'd been found culpable under Title IX for writing an essay and gone public about it, I suspect there would have been a national outcry, and the Title IX enterprise would have faced the public scrutiny it should be getting and isn't. In the end, I wondered if my investigators weren't clearing me as much as they were shoring up Title IX.

To that extent, part of me wished they'd been a little less thorough. I became the poster person for Title IX overreach and threats to academic freedom, because I was the "good" respondent. But what about all the incredible overreach still going on behind closed doors?

The second thing that surprised me was what terrible readers my complainants were. These were graduate students, aspiring philosophers, yet they utterly misconstrued entire passages of the essay: inventing affronts that weren't there, and convincing themselves that scattered phrases in the essay were secretly about Hartley that had nothing to do with her. Even if Hartley strongly *felt* the lines referred to her, the report carefully asserted, they didn't. I recall the term "reasonable person" being used multiple times.

Both complainants would continue to insist, in the weeks after the resolution and over the course of the next year and a half, in anonymous online posts—"One of the Kipnis Complainants Speaks Out"—and elsewhere (including ironically, in a widely circulated draft of a PEN report on campus speech, which liberally quotes one of my complainants), that the Title IX case against me was never about trying to stifle my views; it was over "factual liberties" I'd taken and my "violation of the norms of academic integrity." I couldn't decide what was more irritating: to read something so inaccurate purporting to combat inaccuracy, or to find one of my complainants asserting, with a perverse, Orwellian twist, that accuracy "is a necessary precursor to academic freedom."

Who were they to set themselves up as the central committee on academic freedom when they obviously had no idea why it matters?

After I came out about my Title IX case, I acquired a lot of new pen pals, some of whom took pleasure in dispatching various bits of insider info my way about the players in the philosophy community. One particularly in-the-know correspondent suggested that a backstage player in the complaints against me may have been Heidi Lockwood, the roving crusader for female sexual justice who'd advised Hartley in the Ludlow case.

I was intrigued, and started to do a little digging. I never did learn if Lockwood had anything to do with my Title IX case, but she was certainly involved in the case against Ludlow, one of the various shadowy figures advancing his downfall. Lockwood hadn't only advised Hartley; she'd also intervened in Eunice Cho's case, filing a rather bizarre legal affidavit, despite having no firsthand knowledge about any of the relevant events.

What she did have was a lot of innuendo about the Northwestern philosophy department, which makes for a spicy affidavit, despite the dubious truth status of her claims. Among them: she charges Ludlow with using cocaine, soliciting prostitutes at philosophy conferences, and visiting strip clubs with male grad students. (Ludlow denies all this.) She indicts a former junior philosophy professor, now teaching elsewhere after not getting tenure at Northwestern, for having first dated one graduate student and then, when that student left town to take a fellowship, suddenly taking up with and then marrying another. (He denies all this.) She also says that the search committee responsible for Ludlow's appointment (which included both the philosophy chair and Professor Packer) had knowingly hired a professor with a history of sexual misconduct. (They denied this—and Ludlow had made no secret of being in a relationship with a former student at the time of his hire.)

The Northwestern affidavit provided some quite stunned commentary on the philosophy blogs. Five different people Lockwood claimed as allies and informants posted outraged responses. The aggrieved junior professor wrote that Lockwood had distorted his life and that the affidavit was factually mistaken and "profoundly offensive." Three others said Lockwood had "egregiously misrepresented" them; another said irately that he refused to be used as Lockwood's pawn.

The affidavit also accuses Ludlow of offering to "pass off" a student girlfriend to another philosophy professor. I wondered if Lockwood had read the sadomasochistic classic *The Story of O* as a teenager too, since I recall that it contains a similarly nefarious subplot. What a shrunken view of female agency Lockwood seems to have. Even philosophy groupies—and there are more than a few, I learned—presumably have *some* free will.

Unlike the pseudonymous Pauline Réage, Lockwood at least signs her name to her stories, though when confronted about circulating pernicious rumors, she typically denies all responsibility; her usual response is that she was merely *repeating* information, not attesting to its truth. The abdication of responsibility seems to be Lockwood's signature move, and not just in affidavits. Women aren't responsible for the sexual situations they enter into either, or so she advised Hartley.

Is it possible Lockwood sees repeating hearsay about people as a form of political activism? I recently came across the phrase "noble cause corruption," the belief that a good cause justifies fraudulent means. Maybe it does in some cases, but it would still probably be reckless advice to give students.

Lockwood tells audiences and readers that she herself was sexually assaulted as a student by her advisor, a philosopher who died in 1996. "He suddenly started touching me and behaving in a non-fatherly manner," she explains, which led to her leaving academia to hike in the Himalayas for fifteen years before returning to finish her degree. She also says privately that this professor later sent her coded messages in one of his published papers, apologizing for what happened between them. (I attempted to read the article meant to contain the coded messages. It was impenetrable, but I could detect no likely secret communiqués.)

One of the philosophers I spoke to speculated that Lockwood

had probably felt more for the advisor than she wanted to acknowledge. As perhaps he did for her: after all, if he was leaving her coded messages in his articles, obviously their encounter was a significant thing for him, not some forgettable fling. Whether these coded messages exist or are a fantasy doesn't matter. They're a testament to *someone's* emotional engagement. The question becomes how much Lockwood is imposing her own tangled story (now twenty-five years past and, one suspects, too calcified to be entirely true to events) on the young women she counsels.

In Lockwood's world, women have no desires of their own; they're strictly the passive receptacles of other people's (men's) desires. In "The Extreme Badness of Silence," an online article Lockwood wrote based (she says) on conversations with fifteen to twenty philosophy grad students, she reports that each of her interviewees was almost destroyed by an experience with a sexually rapacious professor. The women report a range of PTSD-like responses: nausea when returning to the scene of an encounter (even after three years), terror at being alone in a classroom with a male professor, vomiting after an attempted kiss, fear of taking classes with men.

I find myself wondering when this version of besieged womanhood came back into fashion. I don't want to sound cavalier about sexually gross professors, but I've heard my own mother describe once being chased around a desk, literally, by her astronomy professor, for whom she was working part time and who was trying to kiss her. This would have been the 1950s. Her hands were covered in mimeograph ink, and she left a mimeograph handprint on his forehead when she pushed him away, she recalls laughingly.

Granted, my mother didn't aspire to become an astronomer,

so her expectations of the workplace were perhaps different from those of a woman hoping to enter her professor's field. But she was in no way traumatized; in fact, she wasn't even particularly outraged. "What ever happened to an old-fashioned pass?" she exclaimed when I filled her in on the responses of today's grad students to similar episodes. About the astronomy professor, she has surprisingly anodyne memories: "He was actually a nice person," she said when I asked if she'd been indignant. I gave her a dubious look. "No, really!" she insisted. (Today's campus statistics gatherers would count her as an "unacknowledged" sexual assault victim.)

Let's all hope that male sexual stupidity soon finds a place of honor in the ashcan of history. Until that happy day arrives, it seems worth asking why a woman of the pre-feminist 1950s felt so much more agency than grad students of today, so much more able to see a professor's idiocy as comic fodder, not an incapacitating trauma.

The Title IX bureaucracy is expanding by the minute, and they're not big on comic fodder either. A recent emailed update from the relevant powers at my university announced dozens of new policies, programs, hires, surveys, procedures, websites, and educational initiatives devoted to sexual misconduct. It's a truism that the mission of bureaucracies is, above all, to perpetuate themselves, but the resource grab is really pretty incredible.

I've gotten many emails from faculty members who pointed out that I was in a position to write what I have about campus sexual politics only because I have tenure. The general idea was that once you've fought and clawed your way up the tenure ladder, the prize is academic freedom. It's a value fast disappearing in the corporatized university landscape, because casual labor (the academic precariat) is the new reality. Adjuncts, instructors, part-timers—now half the profession, according to the American Association of University Professors—simply don't have the same intellectual liberties, practically speaking.

What's being lost, along with job security, is the ability to publish ideas that go against the grain or take unpopular positions. With students increasingly regarded as customers and consumer satisfaction paramount, you'd better avoid controversy if you're on a renewable contract. Factor in the accusatory mania and the intellectual incursions of the Title IX troops, and self-censorship now rules the land. Even those *with* tenure fear getting caught up in some horrendous disciplinary process with ad hoc rules and outcomes.

You can mock academic culture all you want, and I've done a fair amount of it myself, but unconstrained intellectual debate (now on life support) is crucial to a functioning democratic society. Having found myself under interrogation for writing an essay, then unexpectedly at the center of the free-speech debate, I'm pretty eager to hold on to what freedoms we have—and maybe even push them further. What's the point of having a freedom you're afraid to use?

Which means I'm probably being led off campus by security guards as you read this. Please consider contributing to my defense fund.

4

F*** Confidentiality

In other areas of the social world prone to abuses and excess, terms like *transparency, whistleblower, sunshine laws,* and *citizen journalism* have credence because they're understood as counterbalances to official or corporate misconduct. Viral videos of police brutality have changed the national conversation on race and policing; documents supplied by WikiLeaks exposed vast misuses of NSA surveillance. The Title IX bureaucracy's fetish for secrecy has so far gone unquestioned.

After I published an account of my Title IX case, my email account quickly became an overflowing archive of bitterness, cynicism, and fury, with people around the country writing to share their own Title IX tales. There were students whose lives had been thrown under a wrecking ball; sometimes it was the anguished parents of an accused student writing. There were scores of professors, some now jobless or fearing they were about to be. There were many emails with some version of the statement "A similar thing happened to me, but I'm afraid to tell you about it."

With those who were willing to talk, I'd ask for more details and often receive thousands of words in response—they couldn't talk to friends or colleagues and were bottled up with impotent rage. They'd been subject to crazy accusations, insulting interrogations, capricious procedures, and then warned against speaking about it to anyone. (One professor, a poet, described the bullying attitude of his investigators as "savage, crazed delight.") They felt alone—because they were ignorant about all the *other* cases, because of the threats about secrecy.

Sometimes I followed up with a phone call, though I soon learned these could go on for hours. I was like the Title IX shrink, able to offer perspective and ease anxieties because I'd been through it too, and had more of an overview. My patients were in the dark. I could say, "There was another case like this at University of _____." We've heard that withholding information is tactical on the part of investigators. Let me add that it's torturous for the respondent.

It's also not reasonable or just. In the spirit of citizen journalism and transparency, let me offer a few illicit glimpses behind the scenes.*

I'll start with a young man I'll call Tom, who'd been found guilty of sexual assault by officials at his school. His case wasn't unusual; it was a pretty typical story. A woman he'd hooked up with filed a complaint charging that the first time they went to bed, while she was performing (consensual) oral sex, he put his hands on her neck and choked her for "fifteen to forty-five sec-

---

* For anyone who wants to consult a larger archive, there are a growing number of such stories in the news, as Title IX cases involving students are now regularly hitting the courts. The lawsuits are part of the public record, often under a "Doe directive"—that is, without names. I see no reason not to make Title IX complaints and findings public too, in a similarly redacted form.

onds." In the following weeks, the police report said, she thought maybe the choking was a dream. Then she changed her mind and reported him to campus police.

Tom says he never choked her, also that they'd continued hooking up for two or three weeks (three or four times in all, he thinks) after the alleged choking. He'd had no idea anything was amiss until summoned to a meeting with campus police, who informed him of the charges. Next there was a hearing with the vice dean of students. He wasn't allowed to bring a lawyer, but he consulted one beforehand, who advised him not to answer any questions. Was this good advice? The fear was that criminal charges might be brought if Tom fought the charges, which could mean hundreds of thousands of dollars in legal fees, not to mention potential sex offender status. So Tom said nothing and was suspended for five quarters. There were no bruises or other evidence to support the charges, aside from the accuser's story. The woman further accused Tom of breaking a no-contact order by walking past her on campus in the weeks before the hearing, which led to his being banned from campus altogether.

I asked Tom how things had ended between the two of them—why had they stopped hooking up? He was vague: "We just stopped texting each other." It was hard to tell if the vagueness was because hookup situations *are* vague, or if he'd been more casual than she was. I asked if he told the vice dean that he and the young woman had kept hooking up after the alleged choking. He said he hadn't been allowed to introduce any evidence, such as texts. He also thought that anything he said would be twisted and used against him, so he said nothing. This didn't strike me as the best strategy, though it was what his lawyer had advised. Tom appealed, and got the suspension reduced to one quarter, though his transcripts were frozen, meaning that even though he thought he'd been wrongly convicted, he couldn't transfer. His future was held hostage by the vice dean who'd presided over the decision, who had no idea whether Tom had or hadn't choked this woman for fifteen to forty-five seconds. Even his accuser had only a dreamy idea of what had happened.

Talking to Tom made me uneasy. He vibrated with barely controlled rage, even over the phone. Was he an angry young man prior to the charges, the kind of angry guy who gets a little rough in bed? Such men certainly exist; maybe it's what the vice dean was thinking when he convicted Tom without any evidence. Or was Tom wrongly accused by someone whose memory of those fifteen to forty-five seconds may have been colored by any number of factors, even episodes from the past. Whatever Tom was like before all this, his experiences with the campus justice system have definitely left him an angry guy who will forever mistrust and possibly loathe women.

These are the kinds of situations campus administrators are pronouncing on daily, around the country, based on nothing but their own suppositions.

I previously mentioned the case of the Big Ten freshman I called Simon, who was brought up on charges for pleading for oral sex from his steady girlfriend. The charges came several months later, when she decided (after a breakup initiated by him) that the episode hadn't been consensual.

At the hearing, Simon couldn't ask questions of his accuser, and had ten minutes to speak. The panel convened to judge the case included staff members from food services, along with the investigating student dean. They asked him a lot of disdainful questions about the physical circumstances of the blow job. He testified that he hadn't been touching the woman during the blow job, so how could he have forced her into it?

Their eventual ruling hinged on a detailed physical analysis of who had moved, and to what extent, during thirty or so seconds of fellatio. Simon says his girlfriend knelt on the floor, opened her mouth, and moved her mouth back and forth on his penis. She said he knelt in front of her, pressed his penis against her mouth, and moved it back and forth. He said she verbally assented; she says she didn't. The panel's conclusion was that since Simon said he was the one who'd halted the act after realizing she wasn't into it, he was the one responsible for any movement associated with the act.

It's difficult to see the logic here, but the panel backed their decision with a Talmudic analysis of text and Facebook messages that the two students exchanged in the months following the disputed blow job, and concluded, through a close reading of the correspondence, that *if* things had happened the way Simon said, that is, if the woman had verbally assented, as he claimed, he would have mentioned that in the texts. They refused to consider what role the breakup may have played in the accuser coming to believe the blow job had been nonconsensual. Rather, "preponderance of evidence" was established because a college freshman didn't compose the sort of Facebook messages a panel of adults think he should have written to support a story he didn't foresee having to support.

Then there are the grad students, an especially vulnerable population when it comes to accusations: they risk losing funding if on probation, or informally dropping to the bottom of the heap when perks such as supplemental teaching are being doled out. I get the impression that grad students are targeting one another for takedowns not infrequently—for instance, reporting jokes made in off-campus situations to campus officials, yet another creative application of Title IX.

One student was summoned to his school's Equal Opportunity Office for possible violation of the harassment and discrimination policy. What had he done? He'd laughed too much at a dumb quasi-sexual joke in a word game being played at a friend's birthday party, one where players match nouns and adjectives from cards in a box to create amusing oxymorons. One person drew the card "Girl Scout"; another played the card "juicy"; a few days later someone complained. (The respondent wasn't told who—again, this is typical.) He thought the charge might have had something to do with competition over summer teaching slots.

I heard from another grad student whom I'll call Darren, who'd made a joke to a group of friends in a bar, suggesting that the new TAs should have an orgy to get acquainted—or he *thought* he was joking with friends, until a woman pal, who'd contributed to imagining who would do what to whom during the protracted joking, repeated the story to the guy's ex-girlfriend. The ex decided that Darren had been "sexualizing" the TAs and turned him in. He was charged with sexual harassment and "creating a hostile work environment," despite being off campus. (There's actually no such thing as "off campus," according to the latest Dear Colleague letter.)

His fellow TAs were rounded up and interviewed, supposedly voluntarily, but actually under threat of losing their TA-ships. Any comment Darren had ever made that even obliquely referenced sex was added to the list of "allegations," he told me, even though the university's stated policy explicitly defined harassment as "conduct," not speech, a definition that the investigator in Darren's case simply ignored.

Darren wasn't told what the specific allegations were until two weeks after he'd been banned from campus and removed from his teaching duties (effectively banished from his social circle, as well). He was never informed of his rights, not allowed to present witnesses, and the investigator refused to meet with him to clarify the allegations. When Darren complained to the university president's office about the investigator's handling of his case, the investigator accused him of violating a nonexistent security code, and said she could have him arrested. After he threatened to sue (a bluff, since he couldn't afford a lawyer), he finally received a letter informing him that he'd been found not guilty, but suggesting that he should change his behavior.

Darren eventually learned, from reading the report, that there was actually no official complainant—his ex had complained, but then declined to file an official report. The investigator herself doubled as the sole complainant in the case she was investigating.

Darren left, and is now at another university. His investigator is now the assistant vice chancellor for Title IX compliance at a major multi-campus state university system on the West Coast, a huge career leap. Someone thought she was doing exemplary work.

For some of our leading public feminists, whether male students accused of sexual misconduct get fair hearings or not is beside the point. As activist and commentator Zerlina Maxwell put it in a 2014 *Washington Post* commentary: "We should believe, as a matter of default, what an accuser says. Ultimately, the costs of wrongly disbelieving a survivor far outweigh the costs of calling someone a rapist." Maxwell was discussing the notoriously misreported *Rolling Stone* article about a sexual assault at the University of Virginia that turned out to be based on a false claim. Even after the story was exposed as false, Maxwell was *still* arguing that all claims have to be believed. On Maxwell's website there's a photo of her with Barack Obama, aloft on Air Force One. This isn't a random extremist; this woman had the ear of a president.

"Someone is out here raping 1 in 5 American women," writes Maxwell. "And yes, it could be someone that you know and love. It could be the boy at the frat party." Recall that the "1 in 5" stat refers to all unwanted sexual contact, not rape alone. Thus, when Maxwell concludes we shouldn't waste time questioning survivors' stories because "the FBI reports that only 2–8 percent of rape allegations turn out to be false," she's entered statistical Neverland. Not only are rape and sexual assault being conflated, an FBI statistic on false rape reports to police is being confusedly applied to sexual assault reports on campus.

Even if Maxwell's stat had some basis in reality, would an 8 percent false accusation rate really be acceptable collateral damage when it comes to students? (The actual rate may be higher, considering insurance settlements to falsely accused male students and the many pending lawsuits.)

The 2 percent false rape allegations has been a huge article of faith among campus activists (and Title IX officers, I suspect), so frequently quoted that no one bothers to ask where it came from—until a legal scholar named Edward Greer published a rather gripping statistical whodunit in 2000, about his attempts to track down the source of the stat. His first discovery was that though the 2 percent figure was endlessly cited, every single citation ultimately led back to Susan Brownmiller's 1975 book, *Against Our Will: Men, Women and Rape.* Yet Brownmiller's notes provide a rather obscure source for the figure: a speech to the New York Bar Association by an Appellate Division judge named Lawrence H. Cooke, delivered in 1974.

Greer contacts Brownmiller: where did this information about the (now-deceased) judge's speech come from? Brownmiller cooperatively combs through her decades-old files—Greer credits her with being "a very meticulous and organized writer"—and sends him a copy of the judge's photocopied speech. The speech quotes the "Commander of the New York City's Rape Analysis Squad" as having determined that "only about 2 percent of all rape and related sex charges are determined to be false." But what was the judge's actual source? Greer wonders. Was there some sort of official report or press release? Greer contacts the then-judge's former law clerk, who cooperatively contacts a few other clerks who worked on the judge's talk twenty-plus years earlier. None recollects any report.

Greer speculates that the judge may have been quoting a newspaper report, and he sets about trying to locate it, combing through local and national papers. He eventually finds a *New York Times Magazine* article titled "Rape Squad," published two weeks *after* the judge's talk, about a New York City police squad involved in a rape statistic–gathering operation. This squad was exclusively composed of police, however—trained in judo, not social science, notes the *Times* reporter. Though Greer can't find any press release on the squad, he does manage to establish that the *Times* reporter happened to be a friend and neighbor of Brownmiller's—she's mentioned in Brownmiller's memoir (Greer really is an amazing researcher). Were Judge Cook, Brownmiller, and the *Times* reporter all drawing on the same unknown source? Brownmiller gets a little defensive when Greer presses her on it.

The answer may be "lost to antiquity," Greer finally concludes dejectedly, though what he's established with certainty is that the famous 2 percent statistic, what one feminist scholar calls a "consensus fact," derives from a single police department unit over forty years ago, and there's no other published source for it.

None of this would matter if fly-by-night statistics like this one didn't condition decisions on guilt in campus procedures or, indeed, the Education Department's insistence on the preponderance standard to ensure more convictions. Greer thinks that as many as a quarter of men charged with criminal rape might be innocent (and points out that such wrongful convictions fall disproportionately on young black men). In 2008 the End Violence Against Women project came up with a 6.8 percent false report rate based on very stringent categories—lying or inconsistent details didn't negate a report; a report could be unfounded and baseless without being classed as false. What makes this entire discussion almost fanciful is there's actually no agreement on what a "false" report is: if it can be baseless but not false, then what would possibly qualify a report as false?

Given the ease of accusation-making on campus, weeding out "false" reports is even more of a rat's nest. Instead of trying, the general view seems to be that we're living in emergency times, and if a few male students are found guilty of unprovable things they haven't done, that's the cost of vigilance.

Those who attempt to disrupt the official narrative, or disprove the unprovable, can find their own lives shredded in the process. When I first published my own tentative salvos at the Title IX machinery, I hadn't yet heard the story of another professor named David Barnett, who'd once been on the faculty at the University of Colorado.* Would I have gone forward with my essay anyway, had I known what had happened to him? Probably, though he's a walking illustration of the perils of sticking your neck out.

It's a bit of a complicated story, but here goes. Barnett had a graduate student we'll call Ben. Ben had been found guilty of "forcible nonconsensual sexual contact" stemming from a drunken, chaotic evening at an off-campus house involving several roommates and visitors, though everyone was so drunk that what actually happened was vague at best. Ben himself had no memory the next day of the events; nor did the complainant, whom I'll call Ann. At least that's what Ann said the next morning to the female friend who'd brought her to Ben's place. Three months later, Ann miraculously recovered her memory and filed forcible sex charges against Ben.

Though they never actually had sex, somehow Ben and Ann were in a bedroom naked and yelling at one another when Ben's

---

* I first learned of Barnett when someone ("Emily Zola") forwarded me the reports from the case.

roommate, Cary, came in to see what was going on. Among the other highlights of the evening were Ann, blind drunk, falling down the stairs; Ann being picked up in a car by her boyfriend; Ann returning to the house later that night and climbing into bed with various of Ben's roommates, whom she tried fondling and propositioning (Cary included), but none was interested. (It's worth mentioning that Ben and Cary had known each other only a week or so, since it was the beginning of the semester.)

The university's Office of Discrimination and Harassment investigated, and found Ben guilty of the forcible contact charge, though they never interviewed him. After consulting an attorney, Ben was advised to answer questions only by email. (ODH had a local reputation for overreach.) The investigators never emailed him. Even so, Ben was shocked when he received the final report, since it either misrepresented or omitted the statements of the five witnesses they *had* interviewed. Ben's association with the university was immediately severed.

The only appeal process involved appealing to the same office that had produced the flawed report. His professor, David Barnett, tried to help Ben find a lawyer, but none would take the case on contingency, so any legal action would be expensive. A few advised taking the story of the flawed report to the press. The other alternative was writing up an account of what had been omitted from the report and submitting an appeal directly to the university's president and chancellor, asking for an independent investigation.

Ben was out of the country at the time, so Barnett spoke to five of the witnesses and compiled a list of thirty-two points omitted from ODH's report, and twenty-one places where witness statements were manipulated, according to the witnesses themselves.

One, the female friend whom Ann designated as her character witness, had told ODH that Ann remembered nothing the next day, and she suspected that Ann was making up the assault story to appease her jealous (and violence-prone, according to arrest records) boyfriend.

Being a philosopher, Barnett wrote up his findings in the style of a philosophical argument. Perhaps he got a little overzealous: it ended up being thirty-seven pages. He may have been a bit tone-deaf: a couple of sentences could be construed as insensitive to Ann. He submitted the document to the president and the chancellor assuming, as a philosopher, that they couldn't fail to be persuaded by reason.

Instead, the university charged Barnett with violating its discrimination and harassment policies and with "conduct that fell below the standards of the profession." They also charged him with retaliation, then hired an outside lawyer to conduct an investigation proving it (price tag: $148,589).

In the course of this investigation, Ann was made aware of Barnett's report and its frankness about her role in the events of the evening. Before she'd even filed a suit, the university extended a preemptive settlement offer: $825,000.

Yes, you read that right: 825K.

Barnett was found guilty as charged, even though the faculty committee assigned to hear his case cleared him on the retaliation charge. The president summarily fired him, though the committee had recommended only a year's suspension. Paying a vast settlement to the student while Barnett's case was still in process (a stunningly prejudicial move) was a good indication of how little even the appearance of fairness mattered, even at a public university.

Sure, Barnett had embarrassed the university by exposing how flawed their investigation procedures were, but shouldn't the investigators have been on the hook rather than he? Colorado has a whistleblower statute; Barnett brought suit under it. The university finally coughed up a $160,000 settlement in exchange for his resignation. (They also paid his attorney fees and forgave an $80,000 home loan.) The upshot is that Barnett is no longer a philosophy professor.

Among the many omissions in ODR's report were multiple corroborated statements that Ann herself had been sexually aggressive toward the male roommates throughout the evening. This wouldn't suffice as the official story; obviously it had to be Ben who was the aggressor. Nevertheless, Ben's roommate, Cary, brought his own sexual misconduct charges against Ann, for getting into his bed while he was asleep and fondling him. This was a problem for the official story. Solution? Ann was found guilty of sexual misconduct—after getting an $825,000 payout.

In other words, Barnett's conclusions were *upheld by the university*; nonetheless, he was out of a job. Ann's penalty for sexual misconduct? Was her association with the university terminated, along with Ben's and Barnett's? No, she got academic probation (a slap on the wrist), a fact much commented upon in Barnett's former department. Plus that $825,000.

One of his former colleagues ruminated (anonymously) about Barnett on one of the philosophy blogs: "It is true that he is not a terribly prudent person. He rather recklessly risked his career, and ultimately lost it, trying to defend a graduate student from an administration that became deeply invested in making an example, in the first instance, of the accused graduate student, and then of Barnett himself. . . . Barnett's real character flaw was his rather naive faith in the willingness of administrators to respond to evidence and reason. (Some philosophers have no sense of audience.)"

Obviously Barnett's fate is on my mind as I write about flawed investigations on my own campus. I don't like to think of myself as imprudent or reckless, but the idea that telling the truth is forbidden if you're employed by a university seems worth pushing back against.

Barnett was another accused male professor whom activist Heidi Lockwood indicted online, by the way—alleging, on Facebook, after his case went public, that he'd previously been accused of sexual harassment. When he protested to her, via Facebook, that this was untrue, she replied that she wasn't herself asserting the truth of the allegation, only that there had been an allegation, and the individuals he needed to speak with about spreading false statements were the ones misrepresenting her Facebook comments.

The flawed Title IX process that David Barnett exposed was duplicated in any number of other cases I learned about: astounding levels of bias against accused men, inventive deployments of the preponderance standard, and female complainants with ambiguous motives. I don't wish to betray my gender, but the premise that accusers don't lie turns out to be mythical. By sentimentalizing women in such preposterous ways, aren't Title IX officials setting schools up as cash cows for some of our more creatively inclined women students?

Here's another interesting story that came my way. An English professor I'll call Jane was teaching a seminar on the Erotics of Power a few years ago. One of her students was an older undergrad, around twenty-five at the time—let's call her Lana. Lana told Jane, during office hours, that she herself had firsthand experience in the erotics of power. In fact, she had a side career modeling for a bondage website. She told Jane about a new documentary about this website that Jane might be interested in, and proceeded to send Jane some photos from it. Jane decided to write an article about the documentary, which was later published in an academic anthology.

After the class concluded, Jane and Lana emailed back and forth about Jane's article-in-progress, and were soon also emailing about intimate aspects of their lives and histories. Perhaps Jane, a married middle-aged professor with kids, was a little intrigued by Lana's lifestyle. Though there was never anything explicitly sexual between them, as she herself later said, "I should have had better boundaries." At one point Lana invited Jane to observe a bondage porn shoot she'd be modeling for. Jane initially agreed—her research area was, after all, asymmetrical power relations—but then thought better of it, realizing that it probably wasn't a great idea to see her former student naked. After Jane finished her article (and a second one, theorizing the similarities between sadomasochism and psychoanalysis), she and Lana stopped emailing.

A year or so later Lana asked Jane to be her advisor for a student grant that involved writing a research paper. While working on the paper, Lana sent out a group email to Jane and other friends with erotic pictures she'd taken of herself for her new boyfriend. Jane, not wanting to seem censorious, wrote back, "Yummy. I'm sure your new beau will be thrilled."

Lana missed the paper deadline and asked for an extension.

Then she informed Jane that she had a new mentor for the paper: her boyfriend (now her fiancé). When she finally turned it in, not only was it on an entirely different topic, Jane suspected that someone else had written it (the boyfriend/advisor's name was on the final page). She refused to accept it, and later told the university Lana had submitted a plagiarized paper. The same day Jane rejected the paper, Lana filed a fifty-page complaint with the university, charging that Jane had engaged in an inappropriate relationship with her.

It seems clear the complaint was written prior to Jane's rejecting the paper.

Jane was called in by university officials; when she got to the meeting, she found out she'd been charged with sexual harassment. After seizing her computer (a phrase that fills me with terror), the officials eventually ruled that the email exchanges between Jane and Lana had been sexually explicit enough to constitute a "relationship," despite the fact that they'd never even touched. Jane, who wasn't tenured, was put on probation pending a disciplinary decision. Assuming she was going to be fired, she took a job at another university. Ironically, her university *did* allow relationships between consenting adults, as long as they were reported to a supervisor. Not having considered the emails a relationship, Jane never thought to register herself and Lana as a couple.

Of course, it didn't end there—how could it? Next, Lana filed a $1.25 million civil suit against Jane and the university. The complaint charged that Jane had victimized her, then reported her for plagiarism. Also Jane's interest in Lana's sex work had derailed her academic future and affected her health. Someone sent out a press release about the lawsuit to local news outlets.

The story got national and international coverage—not exactly pleasant for Jane. The university settled with Lana for $30,000 while spending some $64,000 in legal fees to defend itself and Jane, with whom they were now allied against Lana's claims.

Jane is smart, insightful, and articulate, and she's spent the last few years trying to understand how she got so taken in. There may be no more adequate answer than that Lana was a master manipulator, and Jane was too trusting. Or perhaps, like most of us academics, her research subject—"asymmetrical intimate relations"—was also her blind spot.

Once again, the idea that institutional power is the only form of power in the world turns out to be a naïve assumption, despite being embedded in university codes and procedures. As Lana, educated in the topsy-turvy dynamics of the bondage scene rather than current campus pieties, proved, to her enrichment. I believe there's a phenomenon known to habitués as "topping from the bottom"; maybe Title IX officers should attend a seminar on it? The powers of the weak shouldn't be underestimated. Or, rather, underestimate them at your peril.

One reason to get rid of confidentiality in campus adjudications would be to cut down on abuses of the process. Another is to initiate an open discussion about what counts as injury and consent. The gender assumptions embedded in these verdicts should also be open to public scrutiny. As it stands, the procedural haphazardness in such cases is beyond shocking—precisely because investigators are accountable to no one.

Even those who've been found innocent get screwed, often spending thousands of dollars (sometimes tens of thousands) on legal fees, and then threatened with dismissal if they dare talk about their cases. I heard from a male professor who can *document* having turned down propositions from a female student who went on to file a harassment complaint against him, complaints that were thoroughly investigated and discredited. Even so, he received a warning letter that a memo was being added to his personnel file stating that allegations had been brought, and that he should avoid potential trouble in the future. Rumors spread throughout the school implying that he'd been charged and let off the hook, which the professor couldn't correct, since he was forbidden from speaking about his case.

I heard from an instructor who had been investigated because a woman approached him at an off-campus bar; they hung out casually a few times and once kissed. Later she enrolled in his department as a grad student. The department chair, a resolute feminist, called a meeting to quiz female grad students on unwelcome sexual behavior; the woman reported the kiss. She said it was unwanted; the instructor says she'd initiated it. The case went forward. Even though the finding was "insufficient evidence" to support a sexual harassment charge, and the woman wasn't under the instructor's supervision at the time—she wasn't even *enrolled*—the chair called the instructor in and told him he was being released, in year three of his five-year contract. He's currently suing in federal court, but worries the lawsuit may cost him his life savings.

I've heard about so many bizarre cases and accusations in the last year that I'd need a spreadsheet to keep them straight. I've been corresponding with a male ballet teacher who was accused of harassing behavior in a class. Male professors who, as with dance, music, or drama teachers, sometimes touch students in the course of instructing them are at particular risk. What happened here was that a student was dressed in a banana costume for Halloween. "I always wanted to partner a banana," the professor joked. He didn't mean it sexually—male ballet dancers stand behind a female dancer to "partner her" for pirouettes. Accordingly, he put his hands on her hips in the standard position for a ballet turn. Everyone in the class laughed. It was a dance joke, he explained. When he was hauled in for questioning, it had become a sexual innuendo. At least he *thought* the banana joke was one of the charges: at the point we spoke he'd been through months of investigation without being told what he was supposed to have done. He felt sure he'd lose his job. He had an enemy in his department, he mentioned, who'd prodded his students to lodge complaints. I heard this a lot: where there are off-the-wall charges, a colleague is often behind them.

I heard from a well-regarded tenured professor and orchestra director with an endowed chair who was forced to resign his position because he had, and continues to have, a relationship with a forty-year-old member of the community orchestra. (He's forty-six.) She's divorced with three children; they'd known each other for several years when the friendship developed into a romance. They kept it strictly off-campus. Then she enrolled as a part-time non-traditional student. Several anonymous letters were sent to his chair, the dean, and the president, threatening to publicize the situation if the college didn't let him go. The professor suspects dirty politics in his department; also it's a religious school, and he was separated, with a divorce in process. It's possible his soon-to-be ex-wife was involved. He filed appeals, but it was "one of those situations where if you win you lose," he says. He accepted a severance package and resigned. His significant other also protested to the dean about being used as a "claimant" in the Title IX proceedings; she was told that no claimant was necessary. She wrote me separately that having her partner forced out of a job over her had been difficult beyond words, but they hope that sharing their story will help make the point that "professors and students—particularly adult women who are able to make their own decisions—deserve respect and privacy with regards to their personal lives."

Sometimes the charges are completely ideological, and your investigators have no idea what they're talking about, but how do you prove it? I heard from a professor at a prestigious eastern university whose teaching assistants filed complaints about depictions of gender and race in readings he'd assigned, from his own area of expertise (intellectual history). He was summoned by his university's vice president of institutional diversity and equity (who was also the Title IX officer) to justify his having assigned ex-slave Frederick Douglass's autobiography, in conjunction with studying Hegel's master-slave dialectic. (I mentioned this to a Hegelian intellectual historian I happen to know who's also well versed in Afro-American literature; he thought it was a brilliant assignment.) The accused professor's grad students also objected to being assigned readings by feminist scholars whose views on gender they disagreed with. The professor was presented by the diversity officer with a list of twenty-seven garbled remarks he'd supposedly made; when he tried to explain the remarks, the diversity officer likened the professor, who'd grown up in Nazi-occupied Belgium, to Hitler. At first he thought she was comparing Hegel to Hitler, but she later repeated the Hitler comparison to the university's grievance committee when the professor filed a complaint. The professor was forbidden from teaching the same course again.

One veteran professor, the recipient of many teaching awards over the years, wrote that he'd been accused of kissing a student on the forehead during office hours. (If male sexuality is, by definition predatory, then even a kiss on the forehead is an expression of sexual predation.) The professor said this kiss never happened; the student was emotionally disturbed and, at the time, flunking out of the program. After being investigated, he was further accused of posting a comment on a group Facebook photo of women students in the program that someone thought was lascivious. I've seen the comment and can attest that there was nothing lascivious about it. During the course of this lengthy investigation, he wasn't told what the charges against him were or allowed to present a defense. He also received a series of maniacally escalating threats from his campus's inaptly titled "civil rights investigator" warning him what would happen if he mentioned the charges to anyone. A few excerpts:

> Due to confidentiality, please *do not mention* this request to anyone else at this time. Investigations must be kept confidential both during an investigation and after it concludes.

You are required to keep this meeting request and the investigation confidential and you may only discuss these matters with persons who have an authorized need to know (i.e chair, spouse, legal or religious advisor).

Any breach of confidentiality or alleged retaliation will be investigated and may result in disciplinary action, up to and including dismissal.

You must keep this matter confidential and refrain from discussing it with those who filed the complaint . . . you are strongly cautioned against referencing the substance of the investigations or the findings—whether verbally, in email, during lecture, or otherwise—even if names are redacted.

I believe the existence of such gag orders is entirely for the protection of the functionaries who issue them.

A grad student I'll call Richard and an undergrad I'll call May, both in the performing arts and sharing an office—she did work for the department—were friendly. Richard had some teaching assistant duties but no grading power over anyone. One evening the two exchanged text and Facebook messages, initiated by May, who was, she said, drunk. They continued messaging on two more occasions over the next day or so; personal subjects were discussed; the conversations also turned to sex. May participated in these conversations, sometimes turning the subject back to sex. On four separate occasions Richard asked if she felt comfortable and whether the conversation was consensual. Each time, she answered yes, though May later charged Richard with creating a hostile environment, saying she felt pressured into texting about sex and had done it because she didn't want Richard to feel uncomfortable and because she was scared about what he'd do if she didn't play along.

A six-month investigation ensued. Nine witnesses were interviewed in addition to May and Richard. One witness was May's jealous boyfriend (someone with sexual issues of his own, May had confided to Richard), who in turn spread a lot of rumors and charges about Richard throughout the department.

After half a year spent examining the Facebook and text messages, the Title IX investigator produced an *eighty-seven-page report* concluding that a preponderance of the evidence demonstrated that the two had engaged in conduct of a sexual nature. The investigator didn't believe Richard's claims that he hadn't made sexual advances to May. The question was whether the conduct was unwelcome. Much hinged on May's assertion that she felt Richard had power over her. Even though he *didn't* actually have any supervisory power over her, the investigator concluded that it was *reasonable* for May to *feel* that Richard had power— even if he didn't. However, she did not find it more likely than not that Richard's messages were *unwelcome*, given May's level of participation in the conversation and her unambiguous consent when asked if she consented. This seemed like a fairly nuanced conclusion, until I read on.

Even though the preponderance of evidence didn't demonstrate that the text messages constituted any policy violation, the investigator was still referring the matter to Human Resources for further investigation to determine if other policies had been violated and if additional action was merited.

Note that these two people never touched each other. Note that merely *talking about* sex now merits a six-month investigation.

I heard repeatedly of investigators going on hunting expeditions, summoning "witnesses," and trying to dig up rumors about a respondent, including about matters that had nothing to do with the original complaint, but about which respondents are interrogated nonetheless. In such situations, the rumor mill starts spinning; all sorts of dirt and agendas get kicked up. In one case, investigators asked a professor about rumors that he was promiscuous. When he said he didn't understand the question, they said that was how his students perceived him. When the first investigation (he didn't actually know what he'd been charged with) concluded with no finding of any violation, investigators told the professor that a second team of investigators wanted to meet with him, because during eight months spent investigating the original allegations (which they'd failed to prove), they'd encountered further potential policy violations.

I heard repeatedly about professors investigated for violations that aren't against any codes, such as dating a former student. I heard about professors charged with violations of codes that went into effect after the time frame under investigation, who were told that no previous code existed. I've heard about mothers instigating Title IX investigations when a daughter is dating a former professor, even when there's no code prohibiting it. And so on.

We keep hearing that sexual assault is rampant on campus. If so, how is it that Title IX investigators have *this much extra time on their hands*?

5

Sexual Miseducation

A PLEA FOR GROWN-UP FEMINISM

Reflecting on recent events in my life, I ultimately came to think it wasn't entirely impossible that in a convoluted and indirect way—like a butterfly flapping its wings in China causing a hurricane in rural Illinois—I got brought up on Title IX complaints because of the booze problem. Not *my* booze problem; I'm talking about students. I never much cared whether my students spent their weekends binge-drinking and barfing into bushes, as long as they got to class. Still, you can't help noticing, if you pay any attention to campus sexual culture, that there's a pretty strictly enforced cone of silence around the drinking problem as it pertains to women and the sexual assault issue. The main enforcement mechanism is that if you mention the connection, you'll immediately be accused of "blaming the victim"—or "slut shaming."

The expanding regulatory net I got myself snared in? I suspect it exists precisely because all the new regulations and codes are so ineffectual at actually reducing campus assault. I blame that cone of silence. The solution to ineffectual regulations? More ineffectual regulations.

As a writer, I've always been drawn to what you're not supposed to say; it's almost a methodology at this point. I suppose I tend to think it's the fast track to unwelcome truths. For example, here's a snippet of the sort of conversation you can have off campus, but not on, which occurred at dinner a couple of years ago with a friend, another writer. We were talking about the campus assault problem, which had been in the news on a daily basis that week. She mentioned that her sister had been raped in college. "How did it happen?" I asked. "She got drunk, fell asleep on the couch in a frat house, and woke up with some guy on top of her," my friend answered. "I guess you couldn't see that coming," I said. We both laughed.

We laughed because we're feminists with a certain shared mordancy about female propensities for self-martyrdom, among other things. And because her sister's story, horrible as it surely was, is also horribly familiar. Yet somehow it keeps happening. As one campus official on the front lines of sexual assault puts it (as reported by Deborah V. O'Neill, whose work I'll be discussing), "99% of the time, both parties are stinking drunk." Estimates vary: a *Washington Post*–Kaiser poll puts it at two-thirds, but that's based on self-reporting, which is problematic, since being stinking drunk often means not entirely remembering what precisely happened the night before.*

I'm blaming no victims here, and shaming no sluts. I'm after bigger game. I understand that the repetition factor has to be framed very delicately if you don't want to be accused of crimes against women. We all know it's not *victim* behavior that needs

---

* The 2011 Dear Colleague letter does mention that the majority of campus sexual assaults occur when women are incapacitated by alcohol, though this is buried at the end of a footnote about something else.

to change; it's the *perpetrators* who are the problem. At least, that's the approved narrative.

I'd like to try to complicate the story a bit.

To begin with, reports about the quantity and variety of what gets imbibed at a typical college gathering, by both women and men, are nausea-inducing. I don't mean that as a moral indictment. I mean only that if I drank in these amounts and combinations, I'd be semi-comatose on the bathroom floor, which is where a lot of women lately find themselves. A typical evening's drinking for a young woman (as reported in one recent lawsuit) might include:

> A "Strawberita" {8 percent alcohol, almost twice the level of beer}, drunk while playing beer pong, then a 100 ml. flask of Jack Daniels {a bit more than two shots} mixed with Vanilla Coke. When she asked for another drink someone offered Fireball, which is cinnamon flavored whiskey. She declined but when she took the next sip of her drink, thought she tasted cinnamon. {After that} she recalls very little—her memory was "like a fog"—everything went black. She recalls being in a bathroom by herself feeling sick and throwing up; her body felt limp, and she couldn't feel or move her arms or legs.

This was, says the complainant, a student named Molly Morris, a moderate-consumption evening; she'd drunk similar amounts on other occasions with no ill effects. She later thought the Fireball may have been drugged, because she didn't remember anything after drinking it, but it's also the case that she'd been drinking pretty fast. It was 2:00 a.m. when she arrived at the party that a male friend named Corey Mock had invited her to. He'd been drinking beer since the party started at eight (for six or so hours) and was, by his own account, "pretty drunk." (It's not reported if Morris had been drinking earlier in the evening.) An hour after she got there, the two went into a bedroom. The college found that the sex that ensued was nonconsensual. Mock sued the school, claiming that he and Morris had been equally drunk and that the school's ruling was arbitrary.

When we talk about sexual assault on campus, the Morris-Mock case represents, by all accounts, the typical fact pattern, so maybe it's worth trying to talk more honestly about *why* it's such an enduring pattern.

When asked (and I have asked), students universally tell you they drink to relax. They drink to forget the pressures. They drink to lose their inhibitions. This often results in women (many, I suspect, schooled by us feminist professors that gender is a social construction) trying to match guys shot for shot in drinking rituals that parody equality, and then passing out first because beer pong doesn't differentiate for body mass. Longitudinal studies of drinking styles observe a sharp increase in "intentional or efficient intoxication" among young women—that is, fasting before drinking or rapidly downing shots, to get drunk as fast as possible. This means a lot of passing out. And a lot of blacking out. And passing out and occasionally winding up with some guy on top of you, often a "friend." Or blacking out and having sex you didn't exactly want to have. (Blacking out means you seem conscious but aren't forming memories, due to diminished blood circulation to the brain, which is why heavy drinkers often have amnesia about the previous night's events.)

Women students, by day men's equals—in class, feisty and assertive, pursuing careers, no one's doormat—too often seem to end up, once the weekend arrives, lying on the floor in a limp heap. It's not exactly unknown that different things happen to men and women who drink, unfair as that may be (and criminal as that may be: no one's excusing the guys). As Sarah Hepola puts it in her memoir, *Blackout: Remembering the Things I Drank to Forget*, "I heard a saying once about drunks. Men wake up in jail cells, and women wake up in strangers' beds."

Still, if you're going to talk about the drinking in conjunction with the nonconsensual sex, tread carefully. One researcher studying campus assault calls it "the 'third rail' of the discourse, something no one wants to go near." Anyone who suggests that women should drink less to avoid sexual assault will be "disemboweled upon arrival into the gladiator arena of public discourse," as Hepola puts it. Those running sexual violence prevention programs (now mandatory on campuses) often don't bring up drinking or dance carefully around it. The University of Virginia's new Alcohol-Wise training module is a typically mealy-mouthed example, devoted to helping students "clarify their choices around drinking habits and attitudes." Agencies that fund sex assault research, including the Justice Department, have told researchers that focusing on alcohol is "out of scope." Academics presenting reports have been told to take the word *alcohol* out of their presentation titles; drinking can be discussed only in the context of "wellness."*

---

* This prohibition may be slowly lifting. In September 2014, the *Chronicle of Higher Education* ran an article titled "Why Campuses Can't Talk About

Having heard so often that one in five students is being sexually assaulted, despite some reservations about the stat, I started looking around my own classrooms—what percentage of my women students had or would become sexual assault statistics?

Trying to learn more, I started making it a point over the last year to have conversations with them on the subject, mostly women students I knew fairly well, and sometimes friends they suggested I speak to. (I talked to a few male students too.) I asked about unwanted sex, sexual assault, drunken hookups. I started by asking what they'd observed or heard from friends, to make it clear that I wasn't trying to pry into their sex lives, which might have seemed creepy, though trained by social media to be self-disclosing, they were usually more than happy to talk about their own experiences.

I hasten to add that this was in no way a systematic endeavor. Also, our campus may not be typical, though what campus is? (Students tell me it's not much of a party school and that the drinking is actually less intense than at other places.) My students may not be typical either, though what students are? Most campuses are far from homogenous: you can usually find sorority sisters who frequent "CEO and Company Ho"–themed frat

---

Alcohol When It Comes to Sexual Assault"; last week the *New York Times* reported in "No Kegs, No Liquor: College Crackdown Targets Drinking and Sexual Assault" (October 29, 2016), that universities have begun taking measures such as banning hard liquor at frat parties or limiting the size of bottles, while acknowledging that every countermeasure seems to meet an obstacle, such as students simply drinking off campus.

parties and anti-rape activists calling for transformative justice seated next to each other in the same class.

Typical or not, what I heard was illuminating, if not exactly heartening. I learned, to begin with, that many of the women, and one gay male student, had experienced some version of non-consensual sex or had friends who had, especially during freshman year. I became a bit less dubious about the alarming stats as I started hearing just how normalized unwanted sex is, especially blackout drinking and blacked-out sex. There's no doubt that plenty of men are having sex with women who are comatose or close to it; are using various combinations of persuasion or physical advantage, or assuming consent where none is given. Also, for a lot of women, this is a standard part of the college experience. To be fair to the men, it can be impossible to tell when someone's blacked out; you can seem completely cogent while being technically incapable of consent.

Yet how my female students regarded these not exactly consensual experiences varied hugely: from infuriating exercises of male power—the aggressors were all male—to low comedy. Some were indignant, some were philosophical; for some, it was no big thing. Students were uniformly cynical about the institutional measures meant to combat the sexual targeting of freshmen women. Our university mandates what's known as Freshman Freeze: freshmen aren't allowed to enter frats or sororities during their first three weeks on campus, so instead they stumble around an unfamiliar city to off-campus parties with little idea where they are or how to get back to campus. No students I talked to remembered their freshman sexual assault training, including the sophomores—I didn't speak to any freshmen—though they'd all sat through it not that long ago. Some vaguely recalled there was a skit.

I still think the one-in-five stat is probably most useful as a lapel pin, but if "unwanted sexual contact" is the yardstick for a student to become a statistic, just call it 50 percent, or even 75, and let's move on from rape number crunching to reducing unwanted sex. The problem is that moving on would mean addressing the complicated realities behind the numbers. Perhaps recognizing the awkwardness this would present, the generally agreed-on solution to reducing sexual assault on campuses is conducting more surveys, because quantifying the unquantifiable is a safe stalling maneuver. Office for Civil Rights, say hello to Sisyphus.

I like to suggest that what's needed are fewer obfuscating stats and more frankness about what all this drinking *means*. I say this because the more students I talked to, and the more accounts of unwanted sex I heard, the more I became convinced that the style of drinking in fashion is a *symptom* in the classic sense: that is, simultaneously masking and enacting a conflict.

People use alcohol in all sorts of ways, and it's easy to disparage them—consider the perpetual charges of "escapism" or "irresponsibility" and the accompanying moralizing sneers aimed at drunks from upstanding citizens. Personally, I don't have anything against escapism or irresponsibility, and you certainly won't hear me arguing against drunken hookups. "Fuck all the guys you want" would be my motto. Just don't fuck the ones you *don't* want, which is where things get tougher, since this requires women actually knowing what they want, and resisting what they don't want. It requires a certain amount of self-coherence, which isn't readily available when one is passed out.

It's not hard to understand the yearning for freedom, however impossible to attain, that propels people into sometimes drinking an imprudent amount. As anyone with a grain of self-honesty knows, one of the great pleasures of drinking, possibly one of the fundamental reasons to drink in the first place, is being introduced to a version of yourself who does things you'd never do when sober, and enjoys them, at least at the time. Yet the reality is that freedom from self-coherence also comes with the territory—and here we have a sizable contradiction. To expect a drunken college guy to have more self-coherence than you're willing to have yourself, in the face of all prior evidence to the contrary, is to treat yourself rather nonchalantly. Not that we don't all want the world to be different from how it is! No one's saying women get assaulted *because* they pass out in dicey locales: I fully believe that women should be able to pass out wherever they want—naked, even—and be inviolable. One hopes such social conditions someday arrive. The issue is that acting *as if* things were different from how they are isn't, thus far, working out.

The solution school administrators have come up with is criminalizing sex when either party has been drinking—pretty much all sex, in other words—and, of course, holding men responsible for sex when both parties are drinking, if complaints later ensue. What a boon for the assault stats and expulsion ranks *that's* been—except that exponentially expanding the potential criminal class on campus isn't the same thing as educating students, which is what we're actually supposed to be doing.

Here's what I think is being disregarded. It's not just that kids are getting bombed and having bad sex, or getting bombed and taking pills and having bad sex. The forms of bad sex are more specific, and the motives for drinking are probably less simple than just "relaxing." Alcohol is an intensifier; it intensifies acting out. Increased male aggressiveness when drinking is inarguably a factor in what's known as rape culture. Men drink and act out stereotypical versions of masculinity, especially men in groups—namely, frat guys and athletes. Men drink because, as one of my male students tells me, "What you do when you're drunk isn't really you." You don't have to take responsibility for it: "It was the booze, not me." And of course guys like to drink because the more alcohol you've drunk, the more "into you" girls seem, he acknowledged. Translation: it helps them combat their insecurities about sex.

And what about the other side of the gender divide? Is it possible that it's not men alone for whom "gender progress" has been a little superficial? Drinking may be a way of shedding inhibitions, but if we can't also talk about the ways that drinking increases tendencies for stereotypical *female* behavior, too—namely, female passivity—then we're being gender hypocrites.

The pattern, in other words, when it comes to heterosexual sex, is college-age men and women getting bombed and acting out the respective gender extremes: men as aggressors, as predators; women as passive, as objects—because what's more passive than a woman in a drunken stupor or unconscious on the bathroom floor?

It's worth acknowledging that gender progress, for all its pluses, comes with a certain level of fun dampening—a "raised consciousness," in the classical feminist formulation. How fun is that? If such dampers are among the first shed by drunken students, maybe we should ask, for the sake of honesty, whether the chance to enact regressive gender stereotypes might be among the reasons for getting plastered out of your gourd: not an unintended consequence, but a motive; not just for men, for women, too. If 44 percent of students binge-drink, as studies estimate, if binge drinking is a great way of inducing amnesia, then the main item forgotten *by men and women both*, is the last fifty or so years of progress toward female autonomy.

The confusion is that college women's drinking comes dressed in the costume of gender equity: women throwing back shots like the bros. It feels freeing to get drunk, it feels sexy. Women yearn to have adventures and be reckless too, and sexual adventurism is still the main envoy for freedom we've got. Something in all of us yearns to be unfettered, even if it often takes a lot of alcohol to get even partway there.

But then we have the shitty reality that the campus venues for such yearnings are fateful. Frat parties are bacchanalias staged on male turf: crowded, dark, sweaty; with loud, disorienting music; and in such "festivities," fifty years of gender progress might never have happened. The atmosphere is so gross that some of my students described getting drunk and doing pills before parties ("pregaming the party") just to endure the anticipated unpleasantness.

Students described the main activity at college parties to sociologist Lisa Wade, in *American Hookup*, as grinding—a combination of dancing and dry humping—with guys coming up to women from behind and grinding their crotches into the women's butts, and willing women pushing their swaying backsides into men's crotches. But it's the men doing the choosing, and the women don't always know whose erection they're pushing up against. In Wade's account, these women aren't being assaulted, they're engaging in mating rituals; hoping to allure high status guys to hook up with to impress their friends. But the line between dancing and assault would seem to rest on next morning's foggy recollections—and, of course, the later appraisals of student deans.* Going to these parties sober is against the rules.

"Fucking hell holes" was one of my own student's description of the frat parties she'd been to.

If college drinking is a symptom, then uneven progress toward emancipation for women (including ambivalences about responsibility for our own freedom) would be the place to start looking for causality. The issue with the drinking is unconsciousness, in all respects of the word. It's not just about taking back the night; it's about admitting that progress is uneven and ambivalent on *both* sides of the gender divide, especially if what looks like female independence and convention-flouting ends up restoring feminine conventionality through the back door. (Self-induced helplessness isn't gender progress.)

Two different things can be true at once: men are responsible for sexual assault; and women who act as if sexual assault weren't a reality are acting incoherently.

Which is where education comes in. Shouldn't one of the goals of a good education be the capacity to ask ourselves why we sometimes act in ways inimical to what we say we want?

---

* And eventually the courts. A Boston College student sued the school after it found him responsible for indecent assault and battery in a groping-from-behind incident on the dance floor during a student cruise in the Boston Harbor; he was arrested and charged by police when the boat docked. He said someone else had groped the woman, and officials had accused the wrong person. But who would know?

One of the dirty little secrets of hookup culture is that a significant proportion of college women don't know how to say no to sex, which is painful to anyone who thinks that, by this point in the long slog toward female independence, *no* would be the easiest word in the language. Instead you hear, in case after case, about women drinking so much they're incapable of saying yes *or* no. It doesn't seem unreasonable to ask if one of the benefits of blackout drinking is not having to decide. In *Blackout*, Hepola describes drinking to ease her doubts and self-consciousness about sex, even if "many yesses on Friday nights would have been nos on Saturday morning." Eventually she sobers up and is forced to ask herself, "What did it mean that I hid when I was sober, and I stripped off all my clothes when I was blind drunk?"

Another way of putting the question is: How do we know *what* we want in sexual situations? It's not a question that's going to be answered by more codes and regulations. It's also not going to be answered by holding men alone responsible for sex when both people are drunk. It's a question that, for women, requires introspection. Some self-knowledge is also a useful starting point, a quality that unfortunately most college kids are only beginning to acquire. (Full disclosure: I'm one of those liberal humanists who think an acquaintance with the humanities is an advantage on this front and should be required of all students before we dump them into the world.)

So what if we try backing off the regulatory mania and tackle a tougher human subject: sexual ambivalence. To help us in this endeavor, I'd like to draw on an essay on so-called gray rape, by a young writer named Veronica Ruckh, a recent college grad, who published it a couple of years ago on a site called Total Sorority

Move. *Gray rape* is a term that's been getting a lot of play in campus discussions. It refers to situations where women have sex when they don't want to, because they don't or can't say no, or because the guy hasn't asked for consent and just proceeds.

Ruckh describes such an experience of her own: she was hanging out with a male friend who had just said (rather cannily, one can't help thinking) that he felt as if she *wanted* him to make a move so she could turn him down.

> *Before I even had a chance to decide if he was right, we were making out. In my state of extreme intoxication, my mind was racing in search of a decision. This was exciting. This was fun. But this was also really, really weird, and ultimately, not a road I wanted to go down. . . . It wasn't until he grabbed a condom that I really knew how I felt. I was not okay with this. I did not want to have sex with him. But I did. . . . At the time, I didn't know why. Maybe I didn't want to feel like I'd led him on. Maybe I didn't want to disappoint him. Maybe I just didn't want to deal with the "let's do it, but no, we shouldn't" verbal tug-of-war that so often happens before sleeping with someone. It was easier to just do it.*

The next day, she lamented that there wasn't a word for this sort of experience: a "weird place in between consensual sex and rape," a place that most women have experienced but no one talks about. She later called the episode "rape-ish," reflecting that "I certainly didn't feel like I'd been raped. But what had happened the night prior was not consensual sex, and I didn't like it." She wanted the flirting, she says, and the kissing and the sleepover. But "I didn't want to go all the way. And that's very hard to explain to a man who is just as drunk as you are." She concludes: "We [women] just feel like we got the short end of the stick, and that sometimes, we have to do something we don't want to do, out of politeness or social obligation."

The column generated a heated discussion (upward of 180 reader comments) by both women and men about what does and does not qualify as rape, including a lot of stories shared by other women about unwanted sex, which in many cases they'd let happen because, like the author, they somehow couldn't say no. ("Basically this is the story of how I lost my virginity," more than a few reported.) Some women don't say no because they fear they'll be considered teases; or they bemoan that they're "pleasers." Some were simply too inexperienced to know what was happening ("One thing led to another and before I knew what was going on, he was inside of me through his boxers").

The gist of the women's comments was that this is a pretty universal experience. The gist of the men's comments was that they usually have no idea what a woman does or doesn't want. Women don't tell them, and more than a few guys complain that if they stop and ask for consent, women get pissed off, because it kills the mood. Most don't see why all the responsibility should be on *them*.

There was a lot of debate about whether Ruckh's experience was or wasn't rape. What wasn't discussed, either by her or in the comments, I noticed, was that booze had impeded her from saying (or, indeed, knowing) what she did or didn't want. Or, to put it in a slightly more complicated way, the booze permitted her *to say both no and yes*—except, the "no" came only after the fact.

The myth of hookup culture may be that women have achieved sexual parity with men. But it's in no way clear that women's *agency* is either on the rise or equal to men's, especially when it comes to saying no. The source of the impediment is sort of unclear—it was certainly unclear for Ruckh (though she's a wonderfully clear writer). A provisional answer is that there aren't sufficient social prohibitions to rely on these days: women actually have to *know* what they want to do, especially since there are endless pressures to say yes. Not just from guys, the pressure to be sexy or "hot" is a huge social factor—don't get me started on commodified sexuality. Those pressures (and self-pressures) loom just as large as guys pressuring women for sex. In the absence of physical force—and it *is* mostly absent in "nonconsensual sex" situations on campus, according to all the data (only 5 percent of assault cases involve physical coercion, according to a 2009 study)—it's not simply men who are responsible for the incomplete progress toward female sexual agency.

I came across the "gray rape" column because it was mentioned in a civil case brought by a male student alleging that his university's decision to expel him for nonconsensual sex was the result of gender discrimination. The same Title IX officer who ruled on his case had given a presentation on gray rape to a campus organization, cited Ruckh's article, and, according to the complainant, endorsed the idea that "regret equals rape." The man's soon-to-be accuser, a woman with whom he'd had two consensual hookups eight months earlier, was in the audience that day. According to his suit, at some point after these hookups, she saw him kissing another woman at a party, and was upset. After the "gray rape" talk, she came to understand that their first encounter had been nonconsensual—though she acknowledged that the second encounter had been consensual.

This same often-inexplicable parsing of consent is playing out around the country daily in secret campus tribunals, and the cases being adjudicated are ever murkier. The head of a well-known Title IX consulting firm, lawyer Brett Sokolow, has occasionally vented in his firm's newsletter about the sorts of situations colleges are now being asked to intercede in.

A female student claimed a male student performed oral sex on her without her permission on October 3rd. He did so again on October 11th. On October 13th, they had consensual sexual intercourse. On November 2nd, he again performed oral sex on her without her consent. She complained about the three non-consensual acts, but not the consensual intercourse.

Or:

A female student was caught by her boyfriend while cheating on him with another male student. She then filed a complaint that she had been assaulted by the male student with whom she had been caught cheating. The campus investigated, and the accused student produced a text message thread from the morning after the alleged assault. It read:

HIM: "How do I compare with your boyfriend?"
HER: "You were great"
HIM: "So you got off?"
HER: "Yes, especially when I was on top"
HIM: "We should do it again, soon"
HER: "Hehe"

In the previous two weeks, Sokolow writes in one post, he'd worked on five cases involving drunken hookups on different campuses; in each case, the male accused of sexual misconduct was found responsible. "In each case, I thought the college got it completely wrong," he writes, adding, "We are making Title IX plaintiffs out of them."

Another way of putting it is that the new campus codes aren't *preventing* nonconsensual sex; they're *producing* it.

There are clearly sexual assaults on campus. There are also hyperbolic accusations, failures of self-accountability, and a crazy expansionism about what constitutes rape and assault. Most campus rape activists, including Heidi Lockwood, now argue that rape doesn't require penetration—Lockwood calls the obsession with penetration as the definition of rape "old-fashioned and bizarre." Focusing on the physical specifics of a sexual assault is "archaic" and disrespectful to victims, she says. Even shifting the focus from the act to whether it was consented to is problematic for her, since it puts victims in the position of proving they aren't lying.

I think she's saying that what counts as rape is whatever the victims *feel* counts as rape, which is increasingly the approach the officials adjudicating the cases seem to be taking too.

I don't disagree with Lockwood or other feminist activists that heterosexuality has a lot to answer for. For the record, I'm speaking as a heterosexual female of long standing; this is an inside observation, not a missile lobbed by a refusenik. Men coercing sex from women may be standard procedure on the normal heterosexuality spectrum, but so is the tendency for women to overvalue men and male attention in ways that make us stupid and self-abnegating. And I don't believe *for a second* that the supposed sexual equity of campus hookup culture has changed anything on this front, despite the window dressing of mutuality.*

My point is this. Heterosexual arrangements are a pact that includes men and women both: male and female desires, male and female pathologies. Gender is a system: male aggression and female passivity are *both* social pathologies that are, to varying degrees, normalized. Changing any element (including reducing female passivity) is going to alter the dynamics of the system. Yes, aggressively disposed men forcing sex on passively inclined women is routine in our culture. But if women can't be taught to protect themselves against such normalcy because *men should stop assaulting women*, and because learning to defend yourself means capitulating to rape culture—well, here you begin to see the two-way nature of the current social pathology.

When I spoke to women students, I heard various stories about guys who wouldn't take no for an answer, with varying degrees of pressure and unpleasantness. A typical experience, as related to me by a friend of one of my students: saying no a few times to a guy she was hanging out with, being pressed with a lot of "why nots," and finally just giving in. She didn't describe

---

* One factor to consider is rising female enrollments—women are now 60 percent of the undergrad population—and whether this changes the sexual dynamic: Do men get away with worse behavior, especially those regarded as high status, i.e. "hot"? Do women eager for male attention act less self-protectively? Male hotness is so volubly prized by women students—meant to signal gender equity and table-turning, presumably—that one suspects the answer to these questions is, unfortunately, yes.

it as assault. She wasn't traumatized, she said. She chalked it up to her inexperience and being a freshman, though it's still an uncomfortable memory.

Why is a "no" not a no? I was reminded, talking to students, how much sentimentality governs these situations. Or let's call it heterosexual sentimentality. Obviously it's not that women want to be assaulted; too often it's that they trust their male friends and dates and former hookups aren't *going to* assault them. Likewise, the men somehow won't grasp that their female friends are sexually refusing them: they trust that the "no," when there is one, isn't meant seriously. It goes without saying that men have to stop forcing sexual situations, and if they use physical force, they should go to prison. But the *emotional* reality is that the mistaken identity operates in both directions, and will no doubt proceed into adult life and govern future relations as well, but that's another story.

Let's face it: sex, even under optimal circumstances, requires a certain amount of psychological resiliency. Being naked, exposed, and physically handled by another human can be destabilizing and not always pleasant, especially when the other human is drunk, clumsy, and/or a complete stranger. If you're a girl, for the most part no one teaches you what to do or how to extricate yourself when things don't feel good. (Sometimes girlfriends are a resource here, sometimes not.) For the more emotionally unprotected among us, drunken random hookups are a formula for psychological discomfort and interpersonal disaster.

Women want to have sexual adventures and make mistakes, but there's a growing tendency, at the moment, to offload the responsibility, to make other people pay for those mistakes—

namely, guys. Women don't drink; men get them drunk. Women don't have sex; sex is done to them.

This isn't feminism, it's a return to the most traditional conceptions of female sexuality. What dimwitted sort of feminism wants to shelter women from the richness of their own mistakes? Their own ambivalences? And speaking now as a teacher, how do such protections prepare students to deal with the sexual messiness and boorish badlands of life post-graduation, when code-wielding bureaucrats aren't on standby?

Some women absolutely do hold themselves equally responsible in such situations, and I suspect these students fare better than those who fall into the enfeebled victim role. One of my students described a drunken evening doing shots while visiting a friend at another school—though petite, she prides herself on her drinking capacity, a bow to her national heritage—and waking up having to ask the guy she was with if they'd had sex, and if so, had he used a condom? She's a funny person, and told it as an amusing story. I remarked that given the new affirmative consent codes, some people would say she was raped. (I said I wasn't pushing that interpretation, just wondering what she thought of it.) She said she would have hooked up with him anyway, though unfortunately she'd missed the experience. She didn't think she was a victim, though did say she'd resolved to drink less after freshman year (and had sworn off hookups because the sex was usually terrible). Rather than being daunted, she learned about herself from the encounter.

Reading the growing literature on rape culture and listening to the activists, I'm struck by how little focus there is, strangely,

on women themselves. There's zero attention on women's relations to men or what women *want* from sexual situations with
them—beyond orgasms, I mean, though the reality of hookup
culture is that they're hardly guaranteed for women. (Sorry, but
does anyone think a drunken twenty-one-year-old man is going
to be lover of the year?)

For instance, we hear a lot about sexual assault and athletes,
but what you don't hear is any discussion of what college women
think they *get* from proximity to athletes, and certainly no frank
calculations of how much abjection it's worth.

One of my students—I'll call her Tania—spoke candidly
about the status issue when it comes to campus assaults and athletes. For Tania, who's black, socializing with athletes was in-
evitable given how few African-American men there are on our
campus, and how many are there on athletic scholarships. This
meant, from her perspective, a thorny set of equations involving sports, sex, and race. Though our campus may be a bit less
sports-obsessed than others, athletes often still feel like celebs
and expect sexual privileges to be doled out accordingly. Tania,
a shrewd social observer, was a bit ironic about black athletes
traveling in packs, festooned with team insignias and swag-
gering into white frat parties to test out their status. There's a
clear difference between how they walk into black parties and
white parties, she said. Male athletes get to campus with a sexual
agenda, she believed, and use sex to assess their status. "Everyone
knows what they do at frat parties," she said, meaning white
parties, while acknowledging that saying this risked playing into
stereotypes about black men. There was an incident not long
ago involving a white sorority girl running out of a room naked
during a party, to throw up. In the room she'd just left were four

football players, all clothed. ("That's a football player for you," Tania said sardonically; she had more respect for basketball players.) The naked woman was passing in and out of consciousness, and the players asked one of Tania's male friends for help getting her home—then dumped her, naked, on the lawn outside her house. Tania thinks the administration routinely protects athletes caught in such situations, and there's a lot of pressure in her community not to villainize black men, too.

Tania and her black women friends have a complex relation to such events. Was there tension about interracial dating? I asked. Not about hookups, she said, but about relationships. When a black athlete has a long-term white girlfriend, there's a certain bitterness on the part of black women, given the shortage of available black men. Thus the men get away with a lot of multiple dating. The black women see themselves as having these guys' numbers, and if the white women don't, it makes them more exploitable by athletes intent on trading status for sex. But some of Tania's black friends have had entanglements with athletes that didn't turn out particularly well either: too much drinking (and drugs to enhance the effect of the booze), which leads to unprotected sex, which can lead to abortions and self-hatred. There tends to be more traditionalism among these students, and the internal pressure of respectability politics. Also, it's a tiny community: everyone knows what everyone else is doing, which takes its toll, on the women especially—as in small-town life generally, the double standard still carries a lot of sway.

The question is still on the table: what do women think they're getting from proximity to male athletes? The problem with not knowing, and with using your sexuality to bargain for it (whatever "it" turns out to be) is that putting your well-being in the hands of a roomful of drunken football players looks a lot like what used to be called female masochism. There's nothing exactly modern about it.

Here's an interesting fact about current educational efforts to minimize campus assaults: they've been useless. According to all the research, including a recent meta-analysis of sixty-nine different empirical studies, there's no demonstrable relation between prevention efforts and reducing assault levels. (Reporting rates may be up in some places, but so are definitions of what counts as assault, of course.) Few of these educational programs have any clear theoretical foundation. Some may improve students' "rape-prone beliefs," such as victim blaming, but that doesn't correlate with reducing the incidence of assault. The minimal success of any of these programs has been no deterrent to continuing them however, which seems simultaneously well-meaning and cold-blooded.

In my forays into the sex assault prevention lit, what I've learned is that there are deep ideological schisms among the experts. On the one side are the "harm reductionists," who want to educate potential victims about how to decrease their chance of victimhood—using a buddy system at parties, not falling asleep with male study partners, and so on. In fact, the women students I've talked to all do practice the buddy system—they travel in groups to parties and try to watch out for each other, though there are obvious limits given the dark conditions and general chaos of the average weekend party.

On the other side of the schism are the "primary prevention-ists," who believe in targeting potential offenders while promoting overall cultural change. In short, harm reductionists want to aim educational efforts at women; preventionists want to aim them at men.

Why do the preventionists think educating women on avoiding assault is the wrong approach? Because, in the words of the communications director of the National Sexual Violence Resource Center: "Considered in a broader societal context, focusing on self-defense places responsibility on the victim to defuse an attack rather than on society as a whole to prevent it." To the preventionists, risk-reduction strategies are victim blaming— why should the onus be on women to stop predators? "The issue really is about men," says one expert, "who we know commit most sexual assaults, and how do you stop men from doing it, not how do you coach women to cleverly get out of situations of harm." Says another likeminded expert, "Society needs to establish a zero tolerance for sexual violence. Instead of saying, 'don't get raped,' which shifts the responsibility onto a potential victim, the message should be 'don't rape' and focus on holding perpetrators accountable." One behavioral scientist, Sarah DeGue of the Centers for Disease Control, was quoted in the *New York Times* as fearing that if we train some potential victims to avoid rape, perpetrators will just rape other, more vulnerable women.

One notices uneasily that the resulting campus policies manage to precisely replicate the supposedly passé social idea that men have agency and women are people to whom things just happen. Yet training women to have more agency is somehow taboo.

Still, there's growing evidence that "risk-reduction" programs targeting women decrease the likelihood of being assaulted by as much as 50 percent, the *New York Times* reports. Women with

self-defense and assertiveness training are a lot more able to sub-
due an attacker (both physically and psychologically able) than
those with no training. Lisa Wade cites research, in *American
Hookup*, that yelling, punching, or fleeing reduces the likelihood
of a completed rape by 81 percent. (Though it's also the case that
women are least likely to fight off attackers whom they know,
which complicates the picture.) Women trained in self-defense
are also better able to set boundaries in sexual situations with
men, suggesting an overall increase in their sense of agency. So
why aren't these programs being universally adopted? Because
risk-reduction programs run counter to the getting-men-to-
change agenda which appears to dominate the assault prevention
field.

As a teacher with some experience of college men, I'd say that
a large problem with focusing social change efforts on men is
that the men most likely to be assholes to women are precisely
the ones most likely to resist being enlightened. Over the decades that I've been a female professor I've had a handful of male
students—four or five come immediately to mind—who clearly
hated me. Not only did they hate me, but they had no compunc-
tion about showing it, even if they veiled it with a thin layer of
faux respect. Whether it was me personally or any woman in a
position of power, I'm not able to say. I'm sure I can be irritating,
though I'm actually not one of those woman professors pushing
a feminist line in class; in fact, I'm probably a little lax on this
front.

Despite my years of teaching and professional accomplish-
ments, I found these guys scary. They were contemptuous, condescending, and picked endless arguments with me in class.
Some of them were good-looking; all were smart and reeking of

self-confidence—I could see how they'd get over with women, especially inexperienced ones. I sensed they weren't about to take a
no from a woman, including a female professor in the classroom.
They could be quite tactical in their one-upmanship. They loved
veering discussions off-track, which is a no-win situation for a
woman professor—if you're drawn into engaging, you look like
the village idiot arguing with a student; quashing the disagreement leaves you looking quashed. Condescending makes you
sound like a bitch, and then all the other students hate you too.
When I was younger and more insecure, I'd get drawn into stupid arguments or try to pull rank. Nowadays I mostly don't try; I
just smile quizzically and nod, though being reduced to feminine
politeness, even when it's the most strategic response, is its own
little hell in a bottle. Whether it was instinct or something more
calculated on their part, they definitely knew how to best me.

Are these the sort of guys who won't take no for an answer at
a party, either? I don't know, but given the thousands of students
I've taught over the years and the steady state of acquaintance
rape, obviously I've crossed paths with a few of the perps. Personality profiles of self-reported college rapists assembled by psy-
chologist David Lisak are said to include the following: lack of
empathy, hostile masculinity, macho/aggressive and controlling
personalities, impulsivity, emotional constriction, underlying anger and power issues with women. They hold rigid beliefs about
gender roles, objectify women, and are usually hypermasculine.
They equate aggression and sexual prowess with their own ade-
quacy. They tend to use alcohol strategically, to select and pacify
potential victims.

Which, one suspects, is why, when women black out in frat
houses—or not infrequently, in their own dorm rooms with male

"study partners"—some percentage of the time there's a drunken, emotionally constricted guy on the premises willing to take advantage of the situation.

Reeducate these guys? A noble effort, but good luck. In my experience, some students are uneducable—not because they're not intelligent, but because they're rigid character types, steeped in self-justification.

Nevertheless: disputing the male-focused strategies is discouraged if not actively censored among the assault prevention crowd. I was interested to read, in a very thoroughly researched 2012 dissertation by Deborah V. O'Neill focusing on the campus personnel who deal with acquaintance rape, an account of the shame heaped on one staffer (referred to as "P2") for deviations from this direction. P2, who had been for decades dealing professionally with the assault situation, vaguely mentioned harm-reduction strategies to a colleague during a case meeting. Speaking about the many women students who reported having been sexually assaulted but who were so drunk at the time they had only the vaguest recollection of it, P2 commented that "you need to educate young women as well about what's out there and what goes on," particularly if you're talking about prevention. "I got my head handed to me about blaming the victim," she recalls. The head handing recurs when O'Neill herself takes P2's passing remark about educating women as the showcase example, in her concluding remarks, of the "unconscious bias" afflicting campus professionals. "Implicit victim-blaming messages have the power to silence victim disclosure," O'Neill concludes her study, otherwise one of the most thorough to date.

It's a lot of pious language to throw at someone who's simply said, in P2's words, "I'm not excusing the male's behavior by any stretch of the imagination, but I do think that young women are part of the solution."

These failed educational measures are leaving college women effectively crippled. Recently I stumbled on a website called Strategic Misogyny, dedicated to "connecting stories of sexism at universities." The first post, titled "Surrounded," was by a woman grad student who described going for drinks after a conference with one of her lecturers and some other grad students. At some point, one of the male grad students started stroking her leg under the table. Then the lecturer put his hand on her thigh.

"I felt quite scared," writes the grad student, "but also frozen. I was in public surrounded by other people, and yet I didn't feel like I could tell both of them to stop touching me. Why didn't anyone else react? I was surrounded by people who taught me and people with whom I studied. Did they think this was ok?"

No, it's *not* okay (though I was confused about why she thought anyone else knew what was happening under the table). Let's all agree this shouldn't happen. Let's agree these guys are pigs. The question becomes what to do in such a situation, because thus far in human history, aggression, sexualized and otherwise, is an unfortunate fact. How can it be that fifty or so years after second-wave feminism became a dominant feature in the cultural landscape, decades after the term *assertiveness training* became common currency, a grad student, a feminist, can't bring herself to say to a man, "Get your hand off my knee"? This is someone training to enter academia as a profession: does anyone think that once having endured the injuries of grad school and finally breaking into the ranks of academia, it's going to be some panacea of respect forever after? Someone has to do a lot better job of educating these women.

The current approaches to combating sexual aggression end up, perversely, reifying male power. It becomes something fearsome and insurmountable, when it's often pathetic and mockable. Look, I too was raised female in this culture and am on intimate terms with passivity and internalized helplessness. I've had the usual range of female experiences and sexual assaults, which is why I feel pretty strongly that someone has to call out the codes of self-martyring femininity permeating tales like "Surrounded's," not to mention the covert veneration of feminine passivity enshrined in our campus policies and initiatives.

What would happen if we stopped commiserating with one another about how horrible men are and teach students how to say, "Get your fucking hand off my knee"? Yes, there's an excess of masculine power in the world, and women have to be educated to contest it *in real time*, instead of waiting around for men to reach some new stage of heightened consciousness—just in case that day never comes.

When I was an undergraduate, living in a first-floor apartment in San Francisco, I woke up in the middle of the night to the terrifying sound of someone trying to climb in my bedroom window. I could see a man's arm sticking in through the window a couple of feet from my bed, trying to unfasten the stop on the sash. I was frozen, unable to run or even move—I had no clothes on, which somehow made me more unable to leave the bed. In my confusion, I thought he'd grab me as I ran by the window. It took me forever even to manage to scream—in my memory, I tried and no sound came out. (Vocal paralysis has provided the material for several decades of nightmares since.) Finally, my male roommate, a law student, whose room was at the front of the flat, heard me screaming and ran in wielding a chair, thinking someone was inside the apartment. When he flipped on the light, the guy took off. The next morning, we discovered the would-be intruder had pulled a garbage can under the window to climb up. If I hadn't woken up, or if my roommate hadn't been home, I suspect I'd have become another rape stat. That memory of being unable to move haunted me for a decade.

Freezing in panic situations turns out to be a common female trait—compare the respective behaviors of my male roommate, not an especially huge guy, and me, frozen in the bed. So, it's not as though I don't understand "Surrounded's" response to those hands on her legs.

In my late twenties, living in Chicago, I took two women's self-defense courses, from a group called Model Mugging, which is still around. Their philosophy is "Crime is an emotional and physical problem." The focus of the classes was on learning to identify and avoid situations where rapes tend to happen, and how to fight off an attacker if you have to, because the more difficult you make it for a rapist, the more likely he is to give up. But simply knowing how to defend yourself prevents assaults, they say: they call this "the paradox of self-defense." We learned how to break an attacker's nose with the heel of our hand, stomp insteps, and fight off large men in padded body suits. Graduation involved breaking a board with your bare foot.

What was harder than breaking the board was yelling, "No!" in the loudest voice we could, which we were forced to practice in every class. It was terrifying, almost shattering, to shout, "No!"—

and even though I've never led a very conventional feminine life, I can say that it rankled me to the core of my self. It was like primal-scream therapy. It wasn't just about learning self-defense, it was about unlearning feminine socialization.

They made us keep yelling it over and over until we were hoarse and (for some of us) in tears.

In my fantasy Clery Act (which mandates "Interpersonal Violence Prevention and Education" courses for all incoming students), *all* institutions of higher education would be required to teach freshman women self-defense: how to yell, "No!" and how to *physically* fight off an attacker. (After a conversation with one of my gay male students, about finding himself in a threatening sexual situation, I'd say offer sessions to at-risk male students too.) Teaching affirmative consent is great—sure, keep doing it until it works. (It's not going to.) Yes, harassment and assault are structural problems; yes society has to change. But individuals can change structures too. If schools are serious about reducing unwanted sex, then get realistic about education. Nobody thinks self-defense training will be effective in every case. But it *would* change the outcome in plenty of cases, and we're doing women no favors by not training them in how to deal with the range of situations they're likely to face.

One of my students—I'll call her Gina—told me about physically fighting off a drunken male friend I'll call Jerry. Jerry was someone she'd hooked up with once before, but she didn't care to again after learning he had a girlfriend at another school. But they were part of the same circle of friends and ended up in her room having a drink one evening before some social event they were both going to.

Jerry said, "I think we should have sex before we go." Gina

said she didn't want to and repeated a number of times that she didn't want to, while Jerry was pinning her to the wall insisting that she *did* want to. She managed to get away from him because she was decisive about pushing him off. She also hadn't had that much to drink. (I asked.) Later, at the event, she was in the ladies' room. Jerry barged in and again pinned her to the wall. Some women friends intervened; Jerry slunk off.

All her friends have had similar experiences, Gina said; it was pretty much the norm. (She was in a sorority; a lot of her socializing was at frats.) I asked if she thought that knowing self-defense would have helped in this situation, and she immediately said yes. She did lodge a complaint about Jerry—not to campus officials, but to his frat president, who imposed the simulacrum of a penalty: Jerry was banned from drinking at frat events for the rest of the quarter. Since they knew all the same people, I asked Gina if Jerry had ever apologized. Yes, he'd sent an apologetic text, but said he planned to deny what happened if she complained. "He put that in a text?" I exclaimed. I said I was surprised his test scores had been high enough to get into Northwestern, and we both laughed.

Politicizing rape and reforming the criminal justice procedures for handling it has been among the great successes of American feminism, though one propelled (necessarily, in the early years) by significant blind spots and exclusions. One blind spot is female agency.

Mainstream American feminism has never been exactly long on psychological complexity. The preoccupation has been in getting society to change, and getting men to change, rather than prolonged bouts of self-reflection. Putting male sexuality on trial isn't a bad thing, but we don't want to turn ourselves into sexual hypocrites along the way by leaving ourselves out of the story, do we?

The propensity toward female passivity is no secret. Women are socialized into politeness, niceness, deference to and overvaluation of men—this is on the normal scale for heterosexual femininity, though not exactly beneficial when it comes to assault avoidance. Yet, when rape activists talk about rewriting cultural scripts and gender norm expectations, femininity is off-limits. In all the literature I've reviewed about campus assault education, I've never once seen the term *feminine passivity*, yet in anecdotal and official accounts of sexual assault, it pervades the scene.

One recent example I found particularly heartbreaking. There's been an outcry because four different women at Utah State reported the same guy for rape to both local police and the university, and nothing happened. It was a clear case of multiple institutional failures. Though, when you read the women's accounts, other aspects of the story emerge. One woman's story in particular seems worth mentioning.

Catherine was immediately put off by this guy's forwardness when they first met, she told a reporter. But she eventually gave him her number anyway. When he said he was coming to pick her up, she said she didn't feel she could say no. Later, they were watching TV at his apartment when he started pulling off her clothes. She did try to fight back, but she was a lot smaller, and he overpowered her. She kept telling him no, and that she didn't want to have sex. He told her to be quiet and let him finish.

I very much hope this guy goes to prison. *He's responsible.* But I have a few other questions: Why couldn't Catherine say no to going on the date from the start? Why would she go to the apartment of a guy she already didn't trust?

This isn't victim blaming. It's grown-up feminism, one that recognizes how much feminine deference and traditionalism persist amid all the "pro-sex" affirmations and slogans, even as women are trying to switch up gender roles and sexual scripts. And that's what has to be talked about, *along* with changing male behavior.

Let me venture a few provisional generalizations. *Hookup culture* is code for women operating the way men traditionally have (scoring, impersonality) in the sexual sphere. *Rape culture* is code for the demand that men suppress their (apparently boundless) sexual aggression and operate according to newly imposed (perhaps more "feminine") standards: asking for permission to move forward at each stage and so on.

Both terms are obfuscating. *Rape culture* mashes together all different types or degrees of unwanted sex, resulting in ineffectual, hamstrung educational efforts. Vast resources are being directed toward useless assault education and prevention programs—call it the "sexual assault industrial complex," such are the fortunes to be made. The whole enterprise is a terrific boondoggle for the consultants and entrepreneurs who saw opportunity beckoning, got in early, and now wage public relations duels with one another over whose dubious prevention strategies are better.*

---

* I witnessed the industrialization of sexual assault firsthand when attending

None of them has the stomach for tough discussions about on-the-ground sexual realities, so they hide behind alarmist statistics that generate the funding that keeps them all in business, regardless of how little effect they're having on anything.

Hookup culture is obfuscating, too. I truly hope there *are* lots of independent women having a great time, but an appalling amount of what goes on is still organized around male prerogatives, including on the part of women themselves. It's not "gray rape" we need to talk about; it's the learned compliance of heterosexual femininity.

If sexual parity between men and women is ever going to be a reality, these would be the issues to address. No one thinks there are simple answers or magic bullets, but insisting that men change first, or that the culture reform itself first, may pass for activism, but it's a lot like the old female passivity in a slightly edgier wardrobe.

---

the 2016 Association of Title IX Administrators convention in Philadelphia, with its array of exhibitor booths promoting all manner of assault prevention "products": smartphone apps, online training courses, web-based platforms to manage sexual assault incidents and reports, and so on. With every school in the country mandated to conduct trainings and climate surveys, and much of it outsourced, the profit potentials are huge. As I passed one booth, I heard the salesman say smarmily to a potential customer, "Are you guys in one of those three-to-five-year contracts that everyone is in?" There's an investigative story to be written about the revenues being generated by the expanding definitions of sexual assault, and what part of the educational pie is shrinking to cover it. (Libraries and faculty salaries would be my guess.)

Coda:
Eyewitness to a Witch Trial

Attending Peter Ludlow's dismissal hearing was like watching someone being burned at the stake in slow motion, except this execution was catered—the university provided lavish spreads of food and snacks, and the atmosphere was surprisingly cordial. The five faculty members empaneled to hear the case were striving to make clear that they were neutral and not prejudging anything, which meant pleasant chitchat at breaks or in the ladies' room, mostly about the food. We were, after all, in the Midwest. Even the university lawyers were pleasant. The whole thing dragged on for over a month, which meant a lot of chitchat and a lot of calories. I was tense, and overate.

Another way to look at it was as a modern-day purification ritual: torch the miscreant, resanctify the community. Purifying communities is no small-scale operation: in addition to the five-person faculty panel, there were three outside lawyers, at least two in-house lawyers, another lawyer hired by the university to advise the faculty panel, a rotating cast of staff and administrators, and a court reporter taking everything down on a little machine. Ludlow had a lawyer (and on one occasion, two). And there was me.

One of Ludlow's lawyers had contacted me a few weeks earlier to ask if I'd be willing to act as Ludlow's faculty support person. This was a few months after "My Title IX Inquisition" came out, and it was still causing ripples. Nevertheless, I was surprised by the request: Ludlow and I didn't know each other, and the lawyer seemed suspiciously eager for me to be there. I wondered if they thought there was some sort of strategic value to my presence—a woman professor-supporter in the room, someone who'd gone public about her own Title IX case and embarrassed the university. I was completely sure my being there wouldn't make a shred of difference in the outcome—there was no doubt in my mind that the university was set on getting rid of Ludlow and the hearing was a formality. I also knew enough about the procedures to know the faculty panel's vote was merely advisory; the provost would make the final call, and it had been the provost's decision to put the dismissal machinery in motion to begin with.

Of course I said yes—it was like being offered front-row seats at a witch trial. Perhaps I could create a surreptitious record of the proceedings for posterity.

In fact, the event *was* staged as a trial: witnesses got sworn in, testified, and were cross-examined; objections were raised and procedural points argued. Exhibits were introduced and numbered. The faculty panel called the shots, at least nominally, under advisement from their counsel, who was of course in the university's employ. I was never exactly sure what the oaths were for; we're a private school. The good news is that it's not easy getting rid of a tenured professor at a major research university, or cheap, which is somewhat reassuring as I near completion of this book. Still, the costly show trial seemed unnecessary. If I'd been king of the university, I'd have taken the lawyers' fees and other expenses and just rolled them into a severance deal—Ludlow could have lived for a year in Mexico on the catering budget alone, and framed the confidentiality agreement he'd likely have had to sign on his tiny living room wall, a win-win for all.

Besides which, Ludlow's two student complainants, Eunice Cho and Nola Hartley, had both declined to participate, meaning there was no opportunity for his side to question their stories, meaning the whole thing was, judicially speaking, an elaborate sham.*

My main qualm about having said yes to the lawyer's request was that from what I knew at that point—I'd seen only the publicly available information—I wasn't convinced that Ludlow *shouldn't* be dismissed. You can't have an undergrad sleep in your bed these days, I thought, unless you're supremely reckless—even if there was no code prohibiting it, and even if nothing happens. True, when I or Ludlow was in school, or even as recently as a decade ago, it would have been no big deal. But in my own inner courtroom, if Ludlow was guilty of nothing else, he was guilty of being oblivious to current realities, and thinking this put me in an awkward position if I was agreeing to be his support person.

We talked on the phone a week or so later, and I asked him point-blank if they wanted me there for some strategic purpose. He said he really just wanted someone there to confer with, and asking someone from his department would have been awkward.

---

* According to Bobb's notes, the two had been in touch via an intermediary (a feminist professor from another university; in fact, someone who'd written angry letters about my articles to the *Chronicle* editors). As to whether Cho and Hartley collaborated on the decision not to participate, I don't know, but it seems likely their mutual allies advised them not to. They would have been testifying under oath, for one thing, and whatever they said could be used in a civil suit.

He was smart and thoughtful on the phone, though clearly he believed he'd been railroaded by the forces of sexual correctness, and I didn't want to start interrogating him about whether he felt he'd been in any way complicit in his fate, though I couldn't quite silence the thought.

What I'm trying to say is that I didn't go into the process as a partisan. I decided I was there for support, which didn't mean thinking there was any plausible defense "our" side could mount. I hadn't at that point read Cho's dubious account of jumping in the lake in February. I hadn't read the two thousand texts and emails between Ludlow and Hartley. I didn't know who Heidi Lockwood was, and I assumed, along with everyone else, that a professor who'd been accused of sexual misconduct by two different students was definitely guilty of *something*. I kept thinking of Oscar Wilde's line in *The Importance of Being Earnest*, when Lady Bracknell says to the adopted Jack: "To lose one parent, Mr. Worthing, may be regarded as a misfortune; to lose both looks like carelessness."

Ludlow and I met for the first time on the morning of the first day of the hearing and walked together to the designated locale. Ludlow had been banned from campus, and it was the first time he'd been there for a year—it felt weird to be back, he said. A few weeks later, after a particularly exhausting session, we went out for drinks at a Mexican place near campus, and I found myself quoting the Lady Bracknell line to him. It probably wasn't the kindest thing, under the circumstances, but I couldn't help myself; I found it mordantly fitting. He didn't get angry or annoyed—he had the slightly removed demeanor of someone on a lot of antidepressants, and if I'd been in his position I'd certainly have been gobbling every pharmaceutical I could get my hands on too. Of course, not having known him prior to the hearing, I don't know what his previous, more expansive self might have been like. Hartley often called him "Charmer" in her texts.

The weakness in the university's case, it seemed to me, was that the most unequivocal charge against Ludlow was drinking with an underage student. But the university hadn't moved to dismiss him after the Cho case—they'd disciplined him, yes, but he still had his job. Hartley came forward only after Cho's lawsuit had gone public and bringing the lawsuit had opened serious holes in Cho's account. Also, neither Bobb nor Slavin had actually found Ludlow guilty of sexual assault—Bobb made no finding on Hartley's rape allegation; Slavin found Ludlow had made "unwelcome advances" to Cho, but he hadn't assaulted her. When push came to shove, both investigators backpedaled on the most serious allegations, and both their reports were, in fact, short on actual evidence. They were Slavin and Bobb's surmises, based on shaky speculations.

To dismiss Ludlow at this stage, the university was thus trying to establish that there was a *pattern of behavior*, between what were, in fact, rather dissimilar situations. Charts were produced to this effect, demonstrating that Ludlow had, for instance, gone to restaurants with both women and paid the checks.

Whatever the weaknesses in their case, I could see why the university needed Ludlow to go away: he'd become a public relations nightmare. When student activists staged a protest about the university's handling of sexual misconduct cases (namely Ludlow's), they did it at the kickoff for a $3.75 billion university fund-raising campaign optimistically titled "We Will." When the philosophy chair had gone to the dean to complain about the pornographic avatars used in Ludlow's course, this would have been the dean of the Judd A. and Marjorie Weinberg College of Arts and Sciences, thus named after the Weinberg family made a "large but unspecified donation," one of the largest in the history of the university, officials said at the time.

Big universities are multibillion-dollar international businesses—our campus in Qatar funnels petrodollars back to Evanston, big pharma contracts boost the endowment (now at $10 billion, the eighth largest in the U.S.*)—and Ludlow was bad for the brand. The provost later denied that any university donors had intervened in the case, but who knows what influence fund-raising strategies (not to mention alumni relations) have on these calculations?

At one point in the course of the hearings, something unexpected happened that reminded me of what can be so great about academia, and what we stand to lose.

A friend of Ludlow's, a feminist philosopher named Jessica Wilson, had been called to testify as a character witness. (Ludlow wasn't in the room for this session.) She'd known Ludlow for fifteen years, she said, first as his student and then in two different departments as a colleague, and spoke movingly about

---

* We developed Lyrica, the nerve pain drug marketed by Pfizer, which accounts for $1.4 billion of the endowment, and the building boom has been incredible. You can barely make your way across campus for all the new construction going on.

him as a mentor and a person. Being around him had been a sort of "effervescent philosophical situation" for Wilson and her then-boyfriend, also a philosopher, when they were all in the same department—when she and her boyfriend decided to get married, they chose Ludlow as the officiant "because he was the most erudite, witty, wonderful person that I knew." Hearing about Ludlow presiding over a marriage ceremony came as a small shock, I think, to a roomful of people who'd been told he was virtually a predator. Here was a smart, attractive, successful woman from one of the top philosophy departments in North America (Toronto) who revered Peter Ludlow.

"The thing about Peter is that he's a brilliant scholar, a fantastic teacher and mentor who just creates a fantastic community, a real social community, which is where a lot of philosophy actually happens." Philosophy is all about the interacting, Wilson stressed. Not only had she never heard a single negative comment or even a whisper about Ludlow in fifteen years (and she would have, she said, because people came to her about this sort of thing), but she and her students had tried to recruit him because "he's the paradigm of someone you want in your department."

Wilson herself was someone who created instant confidence. She was honest, incredibly well spoken, deeply intelligent. I got the sense that the faculty panel saw her as one of their own after the parade of administrators and lawyers delivering canned stories in formulaic language. Wilson's was also a far more convivial view of professor-student relations than the predatory scene sketched in Bobb's Title IX report. Indeed, Wilson's boyfriend (now husband) had been a junior professor in the same department when she was a grad student, and she hadn't suffered any particular consequences. "In fact, I think I held most of the power in that relationship. Still do," she said, laughing. They'd been married thirteen years. Of course, her then-boyfriend had been a mentor to her, she told the faculty panel, because they were all in an intellectual community together. Mentorship isn't a top-down enterprise, she said; it's a community held together by a lot of late-night socializing and drinking and gabbing. Where Bobb painted Ludlow offering to co-author a paper with Hartley as a manipulative scheme, Wilson said co-authorship between professors and grad students was a regular practice. As was sharing unpublished papers, another of Hartley and Bobb's indictments of Ludlow.

Wilson also sharply rebutted Hartley's charge, reiterated by Bobb, that Ludlow was an intellectual bully. "That's just absurd. He is the most tolerant, low-key guy you could ever hope to meet. His basic nature is completely live-and-let-live." When asked if Ludlow was sad and lonely (Hartley's characterization in the report), Wilson practically snorted. "He's one of the most social and socially adept people I've ever known." He loved to go out and usually paid for dinner (there was some family money). The entire time they'd known each other he'd never asked for anything in return.

Bobb had charged that Ludlow's buying Hartley dinners was part of his efforts to exert influence over her. The university's lawyers, too, were saying it was part of a predatory pattern. "I've never seen anything to indicate that there was any kind of manipulation there," Wilson countered. Describing herself as "crazy feminist," she went on to say that she herself had been sexually harassed—one of her professors had tried to put his tongue down her throat. She'd also been raped, and been the subject of an attempted rape. "I know what it's like to be a subject of predation and abuse," she said. "I'm very sensitive to those issues. If Peter had a predator bone in his body, I would know it."

The faculty committee was paying close attention; Wilson seemed like someone incapable of bullshit. On the subject of Ludlow's dating history, she was equally frank. Yes, Ludlow had dated younger women—but her own husband was twelve years younger than she was. "Does that make me a predator?" she asked. Focusing on age differences was ageist, she pointed out. Ludlow was actively pursued by women of all ages because he was charming and magnetic. "I mean, I saw him in a relationship with someone for three years who looked like Taylor Swift, was twenty-five years younger than he was, and brilliant." (This was the former student referred to in Heidi Lockwood's affidavit; she and Wilson had become friends.) Ludlow wasn't necessarily the one pursuing younger women. "My experience is that he had to kind of be pushing women away a lot, as an internationally renowned scholar who's like the epitome of cool."

Wilson had explained to the faculty panel that much of her own work focused on what she called "inference to the best explanation," which means, as I understood it: how do you know what happened when you yourself didn't see it happen? This was exactly the question the faculty committee was grappling with, and Wilson took on their dilemma directly—which was where the wonderful part came.

Using her own philosophical research as the springboard, she said that Ludlow's having had a relationship with a younger woman *wasn't* something that "in an inference to the best explanation" had to be explained by his having Svengali-like power over her. The allegation that he was some kind of weird predator was simply incompatible with what she knew, so there must be an alternative plausible explanation. "What I can tell you, from my experience of Peter, is there's no inference to the best explanation according to which what's alleged to have happened, did, in fact, happen."

"But it's an undisputed fact that the undergraduate student did sleep in Ludlow's bed," one of the panelists said to Wilson, almost pleadingly.

The dismissal hearing had suddenly become an impromptu philosophy seminar, with the faculty panel turning to Wilson as the guide who might lead them out of their own epistemological wilderness, away from the forest of documents—they each had several massive binders in front of them, containing thousands of pages of photocopies—and the wasteland of the official reports.

"We can do the philosophy on this," she assured the panel. "There are two things I would say. One is pragmatic, the other is principle. Let's say I wish Peter hadn't done that [had an undergrad student sleep in his bed], because it was going to invite exactly the kind of rush to judgment that it did, notwithstanding that there was nothing wrong in principle with that happening." This was the pragmatic side of things, she meant.

But as far as principles, the undergrad was an adult, Wilson said. She had free will; she'd engaged in the events of the evening of her own free will—in fact, she had initiated them, according to the transcript Wilson had read. It looked to her like "the arrow of pressure was coming from her at least as much as him, but, again, I wasn't there." She was being scrupulous about not exceeding the limits of what she called her "epistemic position." From the panelists' rapt expressions, Wilson's intellectual crispness was like a momentary foothold.

"But the second thing that colors my response is just—how can I put this? It's kind of like the Kantian test, where you say, what if everyone did it? From my epistemic position, I do know that there are predators out there, but I don't believe Peter is one of them."

"But how do you determine the intent of a relationship that happens between a faculty and a first-year graduate student?" a committee member asked. "On what basis do you determine whether the intent was predatory or romantic?"

Wilson acknowledged that it was a huge question. "Part of being in an epistemic position is that we have a responsibility to consider alternative explanations, especially when someone's life and career are on the line. It's our responsibility to look very carefully at this kind of allegation and ask yourself: could there be an alternative explanation?"

One panelist pressed her about the "unwelcome behavior" Wilson had described on the part of her own professor. "Isn't the student's view of what happened the most relevant factor in deciding when lines have been crossed?"

Like a great teacher, Wilson flipped the question around. She'd been speaking from her own experience, she pointed out. Yet didn't the panelists have to ask whether she was telling the truth? They hadn't been there, so how would they know? And if she were being entirely honest, she herself wasn't sure if the disturbing thing was a professor trying to kiss her, or simply that she was getting unwanted attention that she "wasn't participating in."

At this point the ground momentarily shifted. One of the panelists said, "And in this case the students *are participants*."

It wasn't clear if it was a question or a statement, but for an instant the two female students were sexual agents too, and the university's case against Ludlow collapsed.

Another panelist quickly countered, "It seems very clear the students feel they have been harmed. That is definitely the message that the university is presenting, at least from the interviews with the investigators: that they feel harmed."

Wilson's solution, again, was inference to the best explanation. "What's the best explanation of all of the data? It's a delicate position. But, I mean—we're aware of human nature. Sometimes a person's memories can be distorted. There are psychological and other motivations that need to be brought to bear."

I think she was trying to remind everyone in the room, as delicately as possible, that people don't always tell the truth, even student accusers.

She added, sympathetically, addressing the panel, "I don't think your task is an easy one. Basically I just want to put my part of evidence on the table, which is that I love Peter Ludlow. I've known him for fifteen years. He's a great person. He's a staunch feminist. He cares about women. He supports women. He mentors them. He treated me exactly the same as any male, and all of these considerations weigh quite heavily in my mind because I've known him for so long and so intimately."

She was near tears, anguished about the impossibility of rescuing Ludlow from this web of shaky accusations and the phalanx of lawyers gathered to end his career. It was slightly embarrassing: there she was humanizing the person the process was designed to demonize. But I think the professors were all a little in love with Wilson right then. She was one of us, and she'd risen to the occasion heroically, transforming the hearing into a symposium, and herself into the best sort of mentor. There were no easy platitudes about victims and survivors. She simply had such conviction in the power of thinking to solve problems that it was mesmerizing.

It probably sounds bizarre to say, given the circumstances, but it felt like there was an erotic current in the room. It reminded me of my own student days, when the excitement of learning made me feel alive in such profoundly creative, intellectual, erotically messy ways—which were indistinguishable from one another, and no one thought it should be otherwise.

The hearings went on and on, and were nowhere near concluding when Ludlow told me he was thinking of pulling the plug and resigning. As his faculty advisor, I advised him against it, but he didn't foresee a positive outcome; also he was bleeding money on lawyers who were no match for the university's, numerically or otherwise. His lead lawyer turned out to be terrible at cross-examination, and squandered every opportunity to construct an alternate narrative to the university's case. He hammered at trivial points, asked multiple-part questions, and repeated himself so often that the panelists started interrupting, telling him to move on. Everyone in the room was completely exasperated with him.

Whatever case Ludlow might have presented wasn't getting made. The faculty panel refused to hear any testimony regarding the students' credibility, including questions about Cho's suicide attempt. There had also been an ugly exchange with the faculty panel's counsel, who could be exceedingly unpleasant, at one point chewing Ludlow out so viciously (over whether he could switch counsel midway through the proceedings) that he was reduced nearly to tears in front of a roomful of people. I'd never seen anything like it in all my years of academia, and believe me, it's not like academic aggression is unknown.

I've had a sense of self-recrimination ever since about not having stood up and objected to the lawyer's tirade. I have this idea that you're supposed to stand up to bullies—that's what comes of forcing us all to read *To Kill a Mockingbird* as children—but I was so shaken myself, so frozen and appalled, that I didn't. That evening, I wrote an email to the faculty panel's chair protesting what had happened, but got no reply.

Soon after, Ludlow resigned and moved to Mexico. I think he just wanted to leave on his own terms.

Six months later, in April 2016, Ludlow reached what he called a "settlement" with Eunice Cho in the various lawsuits still going on between them. Cho dropped her gender violence suit against him. Ludlow dropped his defamation suit against her, and he paid her, as he put it to me on the phone, "zero dollars." Nor did he pay any money to anyone associated with her. There was also no confidentiality agreement.

I pondered this. "What did you have on her?" I asked. "The deposition?" I was guessing she'd perjured herself, his side had been able to prove it, and he was threatening to use it. "More," he said cryptically, which was when I remembered the police report with the wild charges that Cho had never made to Slavin. Ludlow wasn't forthcoming when I tried to pin him down, but filing a false police report is a Class 4 felony in Illinois. If she lied to the police, Cho could have faced criminal charges.

Along with a statement on the settlement, Ludlow released and quoted from the letter Cho had sent, via her lawyer, to the faculty panel in the dismissal hearing explaining why she was declining to participate. It was an exceedingly odd letter. After reflection, Cho wrote, she'd decided that she didn't trust Northwestern's "ends, means, or motives," and the university did "not now have my support in its efforts to terminate Professor Ludlow." The "contentious litigation" between her and Ludlow had become "a significant fire that has grown to engulf everyone and everything with any connection to the people or events involved."

Also, she'd had an epiphany: Northwestern hadn't operated or conducted itself in good faith, and its "inner machinations" had been driven by a singular motive: protection and preservation of the institution at all costs. She herself needed to reexamine "this long road in which Northwestern somehow had input into my decision-making," adding that Northwestern had "opted to play both ends against the middle, and so it will now find itself alone." She asked the faculty panel to consider a "peaceful, restorative, universal resolution."

To call this statement convoluted is a massive understatement, because, if the findings in her case had been faulty, the fault lay in our Title IX officer *believing Cho's story*. A cynical reading might be that having effectively bankrupted Ludlow, she thought she had a better chance of getting money out of the university, and was hoping it was this "restorative" resolution the faculty panel would recommend.

Still, I had a hard time understanding what Cho could possibly hold Northwestern responsible for. As far as I could see, the university had merely tried to stay in compliance with the incoherent directives issued by the Department of Education, an agency of our elected government—even if that meant trying to fire a professor by using as evidence the statements of a student who'd already cast doubt on the reliability of her own statements.

I'd have liked to know how many hundreds of thousands of dollars it had cost Ludlow to get to this "resolution," but I didn't have the heart to ask.

And the cost to the university? It would be fascinating to know how much was spent on this case, and how many millions of dollars annually go toward attempting to stay off the OCR watchlist, but such information isn't made publicly available.

Sifting through the mountains of documents and notes I'd accumulated on Ludlow's case as I was finishing this book, I noticed something I hadn't seen before. In the online article of Heidi Lockwood's I mentioned earlier, "The Extreme Badness of Silence," I saw that the date it was posted, March 25, 2014, was less than a week after Nola Hartley met with Patricia Bobb, the Title IX investigator, on March 19, 2014.

In this article, Lockwood writes that she'd had fifteen to twenty conversations in the past month with "survivors of faculty-student sexual misconduct," whom she quotes anonymously. According to Bobb's notes, Hartley had conferred with Heidi Lockwood shortly before Bobb and Hartley's meeting. It seemed likely, given the overlapping time frames, that some of the anonymous quotes in the article would have come from Hartley.

With that in mind, a quote in a section labeled "Confusion and Hatred" caught my eye:

"It was consensual, but I didn't have any choice—he has too much power in the discipline—and at points I have hated him so much for taking advantage of the power asymmetry that I have plotted revenge against him."

The reason the quote caught my eye is that it seemed so similar to how Hartley had framed her relationship with Ludlow to Bobb, as Bobb reports:

She had begun to realize that her relationship with Ludlow had not been "consensual" because of the power differential between them and that he had manipulated and taken advantage of her.

Similar, though not identical. Still, in both quotes, the speaker has been taken advantage of. There are power differentials or asymmetries. The relationship was either not consensual or consensual minus a choice—that is, not consensual. The man in question has a lot of power in the philosophy discipline.

The big difference is the admission, to Lockwood, that the speaker had plotted revenge, a theme absent in the passage from Bobb's report.

Did both passages refer to Ludlow? There's no way to say. Still, it left me wondering: *did* Hartley hate Ludlow enough to take revenge? A false or pumped-up rape accusation would definitely do the trick—even if unprovable, it would be a career ender.

No doubt we all fantasize about catastrophic fates for hated enemies and exes, though I noticed that Lockwood's unnamed grad student doesn't say she *fantasized* about taking revenge against her foe. She says she *plotted* revenge.

If, for Hartley's advisor Heidi Lockwood, activism sometimes entails circulating false information about people—as Lockwood did against a slew of outraged Northwestern faculty in the affidavit she filed in Eunice Cho's case—would a false or pumped-up rape charge be justified, too, to get a supposed predator ousted from academia?

Again, no way to say. What can be said is that Hartley went from believing her relationship with Ludlow had been consensual and that he had no power over her, to believing the opposite a few years later, and these newfound beliefs duplicate Heidi Lockwood's public statements on consent and power. During their relationship, Hartley texted Ludlow: "I haven't taken any classes from you. You're not grading my shit." To Bobb, two years later, she said, "Peter was my teacher."

He wasn't and never had been, but maybe she saw it as a justified falsehood.

"Are the accusers always holy now?" demands the accused witch John Proctor (soon to be executed) in Miller's *The Crucible*. On campus, the answer is yes.

I said earlier that Ludlow's case was practically Shakespearean. The more I shook the bushes and peeked behind curtains, the more shadowy figures and agendas seemed to keep revealing themselves: schemers and liars shaping events from offstage, Professor X and Heidi Lockwood stirring the cauldron, broken friendships, reneged engagements, pornographic avatars, and the competition over women; the proximity of love and hate, the oscillation between injury and aggression, the forbidden eros between teachers and students—and, of course, the familiar fiction of the virtuous maiden.

Who knows how many other "clear-cut" campus guilty verdicts would turn out to be a lot murkier if they weren't immune from public scrutiny?

All this being said, as I weigh the evidence in my own inner courtroom, I can understand why the university had to jettison Ludlow. Personally, I don't think he abused his power. The problem was that he didn't share the conception of power in vogue in academic precincts. (Neither do I, and may soon be clinging to gainful employment by my fingernails for that reason too.) Yes, Ludlow was guilty—though not of what the university charged him with. His crime was thinking that women over the age of consent have sexual agency, which has lately become a heretical view, despite once being a crucial feminist position. *Of course* the community had to expel him. That's what you do with heretics.

Still, the history of purification rituals is a pretty squalid one. Heading down this path once again requires a lot of historical amnesia from everyone involved. That college campuses should be where history goes to be forgotten is depressing on all levels, not least when it comes to the future of higher education—and freedoms of every stripe.

Acknowledgments

If there's one person to blame for this book, it's Jean Tamarin, who solicited me to write a "no-holds-barred" essay on campus sexual politics for *The Chronicle of Higher Education,* then when I said no (I didn't think I had much to say), cajoled and flattered me until I yielded, was a shrewd editor, and then a great pal when things took an unexpected turn. So was her boss, Evan Goldstein, and it was a pleasure to work with such an intrepid duo.

I'm grateful to the many students and professors who shared their often difficult experiences with me. I spoke to a number of philosophers who gave me insights about the field and the players; also with countless other academics and administrators—I'll do you all the return favor of not naming you. Thank you to my colleague, Stephen Eisenman, for going to the mat during the Title IX process. Peter Ludlow entrusted me with his story with no conditions, nor did he ask to vet the manuscript.

My thanks to those who read drafts of the book-in-progress: Lawrence Weschler gave it a rigorous and pointed analysis, Bruce Robbins combed through it like a mother gorilla picking nits off her offspring, and my dad, Len Kipnis, is always my best early reader and booster. Thank you to Sara Bershtel for helping me figure out the story (and for overall wonderfulness), and to Valerie Monroe, Anna McCarthy, and Phyllis Kipnis for camaraderie and counsel.

My editor, Gail Winston, was a terrific surgeon and the sharpest of interlocutors: my deepest gratitude. Thanks to my agent, PJ Mark, who helped shape the book after some embarrassing early struggles with tone. And a large thank-you to David Hirshey.

My sweetheart, Jim Livingston, read fifty drafts and had five thousand conversations about them (and ancillary life events), and made this book far smarter than it might otherwise have been, and me far happier than would seem possible.

I'm also grateful to Northwestern University, which has been kind enough to employ me for many years. Our president, Morton Schapiro, has been outspoken about protecting academic freedom while soothing the constituencies who would axe it, which is a tough balancing act. My dean, Barbara O'Keefe, is a savvy realist and another tough balancer. It's worth saying that I felt able to write a combustible essay about the Title IX process because I had faith that my university (unlike many others these days), would back my right to write what I thought—whether or not anyone agreed with me—which proved to be the case. Despite our occasional disagreements, I believe it's a place that strives to achieve the ideals of a great university.

Selected Sources

Anderson, Linda A., and Susan C. Whiston. "Sexual Assault Education Programs: A Meta-Analytic Examination of Their Effectiveness." *Psychology of Women Quarterly* 29 (2005): 374–88.

Bernstein, Elizabeth. "Carceral Politics as Gender Justice? The "Traffic in Women" and Neoliberal Circuits of Crime, Sex, and Rights." *Theory and Society* 41, no. 3 (May 2012): 233–59.

Clark, Anne E., and Andrea L. Pino. *We Believe You: Survivors of Campus Sexual Assault Speak Out.* New York: Henry Holt and Company, 2016.

Demos, John Putnam. *Entertaining Satan: Witchcraft and the Culture of Early New England.* Oxford, U.K.: Oxford University Press, 1982.

Echols, Alice. *Daring to Be Bad: Radical Feminism in America 1967–1975.* Minneapolis: University of Minnesota Press, 1989.

Ferrante, Elena. *The Story of a New Name.* Translated by Ann Goldstein. New York: Europa Editions, 2013.

Gersen, Jacob and Jeannie Suk. "The Sex Bureaucracy." *California Law Review* 881 (2016): 881–948.

Gibbons, Roberta E. "The Evaluation of Campus-Based Gender Violence Prevention Programming: What We Know about Program Effectiveness and Implications for Practitioners." National Online Resource Center on Violence Against Women, January 2013, http://www.vawnet.org/.

Gidycz, Christine A., Lindsay M. Orchowski, and Alan D. Berkowitz. "Preventing Sexual Aggression Among College Men: An Evaluation of a Social Norms and Bystander Intervention Program." *Violence Against Women* 17, no. 6 (June 2011): 720–42.

Ginsberg, Benjamin. *The Fall of the Faculty: The Rise of the All-Administrative University and Why It Matters* (2nd edition) Oxford, U.K.: Oxford University Press, 2011.

Goldberg, Michelle. "This Professor Was Fired for Saying 'Fuck No' in Class." *The Nation*, July 2, 2015.

Greer, Edward. "The Truth Behind Legal Dominance Feminism's Two Percent False Rape Claim Figure." *Loyola Law Review* 33, no. 3/3 (2000): 947–72.

Hartocollis, Anemona. "Colleges Spending Millions to Deal with Sexual Misconduct Complaints." *New York Times*, March 29, 2016.

Hoffman, Jan. "College Rape Prevention Program Proves a Rare Success." *New York Times*, June 11, 2015, A15.

Krebs, Christopher P., et al. "The Campus Sexual Assault Study: Final Report." www.ncjrs.gov/pdffiles1/nij/grants/221153.pdf.

———. "College Women's Experiences with Physically Forced, Alcohol-or Other Drug–Enabled, and Drug-Facilitated Sexual Assault Before and Since Entering College." *Journal of American College Health* 57, no. 6 (2009): 639–47.

Law, Victoria. "Against Carceral Feminism." *Jacobin*, October 17, 2014.

Lisak, David, et al. "False Allegations of Sexual Assault: An Analysis of Ten Years of Reported Cases. *Violence Against Women* 16, no. 12 (2010): 1318–34.

McMurtrie, Beth. "Why Colleges Haven't Stopped Binge Drinking." *New York Times*, December 15, 2014.

O'Neill, Deborah V. "Responding to College Campus Acquaintance Rape: Contextual Issues and the Challenge of Inter-Organizational Collaboration" (2012). Doctorate in Social Work Dissertations. Paper 24. http://repository.upenn.edu/edissertations_sp2/24/.

Pryor, Douglas W., and Marion R. Hughes. "Fear of Rape Among College Women: A Social Psychological Analysis. *Violence and Victims* 28, no. 3 (2013): 443–65.

Ruckh, Veronica. "Is It Possible That There Is Something in Between Consensual Sex and Rape . . . and That It Happens to Almost Every Girl Out There?" Total Sorority Move (website), September 11, 2014.

Schmidt, Peter. "Accusations of Student Harassment Leave Professors Feeling Vulnerable." *Chronicle of Higher Education*, April 2, 2015.

Senn, Charlene Y. "Sexual Assault Resistance Education for University Women: Study Protocol for a Randomized Controlled Trial." *BMC Women's Health* 13, no. 25 (2013): 1–13.

Ullman, Sarah E. "A 10-Year Update of 'Review and Critique of Empirical Studies of Rape Avoidance.'" *Criminal Justice and Behavior* 34, no. 3 (March 2007): 411–29.

United States Department of Education. Office for Civil Rights. "Dear Colleague Letter: Sexual Violence," April 4, 2011. http://www2.ed.gov/about/offices/list/ocr/letters/colleague-201104.html.

Villalobos, J. Guillermo, Deborah Davis, and Richard A. Leo. "His Story, Her Story: Sexual Miscommunication, Motivated Remembering, and Intoxication as Pathways to Honest False Testimony Regarding Sexual Consent." In R. Burnett, ed., *Vilified: Wrongful Allegations of Sexual and Child Abuse.* Oxford, U.K.: Oxford University Press, 2016.

Wade, Lisa. *American Hookup: The New Culture of Sex on Campus.* New York: Norton, 2017.

Willis, Ellen (ed. Nona Willis Aronowitz). *The Essential Ellen Willis.* Minneapolis: University of Minnesota Press, 2014.

Wilson, Robin. "A Professor, a Graduate Student, and 2 Careers Derailed." *Chronicle of Higher Education*, June 19, 2015.

———. "Why Campuses Can't Talk About Alcohol When It Comes to Sexual Assault." *Chronicle of Higher Education*, September 4, 2014.

Yoffe, Emily. "The College Rape Overcorrection." *Slate*, December 7, 2014.

Zimmerman, Eilene. "Campuses Struggle with Approaches for Preventing Sexual Assault." *New York Times*, June 22, 2016, F2.

About the Author

LAURA KIPNIS is a cultural critic and a professor at Northwestern University, where she teaches filmmaking. She's the author of six previous books, including *Against Love: A Polemic* and *Men: Notes from an Ongoing Investigation*. She has received fellowships from the Guggenheim Foundation and Yaddo, among others, and has written for *Slate, Harper's Magazine*, the *New York Times Magazine*, the *New York Times Book Review*, and *Bookforum*. Her essay "Sexual Paranoia Strikes Academe" was included in *The Best American Essays 2016*, edited by Jonathan Franzen. She lives in New York and Chicago.